UNDAMNED

*My Escape
from the Old Testament*

L. E. KINZIE

For my children. May they never be estranged from themselves.

TABLE OF CONTENTS

Introduction

CHAPTER ONE
Jesus, Are You a Brand?

CHAPTER TWO
The Church of the Immaculate Hamburger

CHAPTER THREE
My Story: Extreme Spiritual Makeover
Part One: *How to Lose Yourself Without Really Trying*

CHAPTER FOUR
Part Two: *The Big Reveal*

CHAPTER FIVE
Spiritual Toolbox for Recovery and Freedom

CHAPTER SIX
Idols, A Remix

CHAPTER SEVEN
Upside Down Faith

CONCLUSION
(The Real Good News)

Acknowledgements

Footnotes

DISCLAIMER

This is my story of religious addiction, recovery and glorious freedom and healing. It is, of necessity, a very intimate and personal spiritual memoir. This high level of transparency and intimacy is imperative to convey my progress and my truth.

However, because I have no desire to tell anyone else's truth, there are things this book is not. It is not a documentary. It is not a biography in any strict sense of the word. All places, names, and locations have been changed to avoid telling anyone else's truth. The word "church" is used in the general sense and does not refer to any specific church with any concrete physical location.

Similarly, the word "McChurch" does not refer to any specific church with any specific concrete location. Nor does it refer to any person or group of persons. It refers to a group of characteristics some churches seem to possess.

Finally, my encounters with "McChurch" and "the Church of the Immaculate Hamburger" describe a series of experiences in several locations I visited along my lengthy spiritual pilgrimage that became a pattern of attitudes and behavior. They do not describe a specific church with a specific physical location.

© 2013 by L. E. Kinzie

PUBLISHER'S NOTE

No part of this book may be reproduced, scanned, or distributed in any printed or electronic form without permission from the author. Please do not participate in or encourage piracy of copyrighted materials in violation of the author's rights. Purchase only authorized editions.

Cover design © by Kim Greyer
Original cover art © by Original cover art
All rights reserved.

No part of this book may be reproduced, scanned, or distributed in any printed or electronic form without permission from the author. Please do not participate in or encourage piracy of copyrighted materials in violation of the author's rights. Purchase only authorized editions.

Printed and published in the United States of America

Violet Crown Publishers

ISBN: 978-1-938749-12-4 (print)

Also Available In Digital Format on Amazon.Com

ISBN:978-1-938749-11-7 (digital)

INTRODUCTION

THE WIZARD OF OZ

I went looking for salvation
and instead found the Wizard of Oz.
Instead of finding
healing for my deep pain,
I found a tiny little man
hiding behind a red curtain.
I asked him to heal my heart
and was handed a Sweet Tart.
I said I needed to transform my mind,
I was given a copy of Left Behind.
I fell to my knees and asked for
Redemption
Forgiveness
Faith and Trust,
and was given Robert's Rules of Order
and a consumer questionnaire.
I traveled far and wide in search of truth,
and the church invited me to a focus group.
It made me sad.
It made me scared.
It made me feel like I'd been had,
and wondering just what was sacred.
So I took a sabbatical from the tyrannical and fanatical
and I came up with a plan
to get myself Undamned.
It was so lonely.
No one wanted me.

UNDAMNED

God had left the building like Elvis
and was waiting patiently in a field of poppies
for me to flee the spectacle of the Emerald City
and the flying monkeys.
When I found Her,
I found me.
Soul intact and Undamned, thank you very much.
Faith intact and Undimmed.
Renewed, tougher, more resilient than before,
I emerged from Hell,
sure that if my maker loves me,
I don't need to take it to committee.
No one else need cast a vote.
She's got my back, and that's all she wrote.[1]

My "religion" was the most destructive, demoralizing addiction I had ever encountered, and it was killing me. It contributed mightily to years of depression and self-destructive behaviors. I was damned. A spiritual zombie. I lived every day in the Old Testament, because I carried it with me everywhere I went, waiting for punishment. I believed I deserved it because the Bible told me so.

I could not have been more wrong. I believed my religion was a source of comfort and joy, but the way I was using it in my life, it was a destructive and debilitating crutch.

After much trial and error and experimentation, I found and began practicing a recovery program from my religion that finally set me free.

Before I could even conceive of an anti-addiction program for religion, I made a pilgrimage searching for answers and comfort that led me to places I never imagined I would go and to a conclusion I was not ready for. Along the way, I literally ran into every kind of church imaginable. I encountered a particular type of church to which I either refer as McChurch or Church of the Immaculate Hamburger because of the way I felt when I was there: like a commodity from a fast-food menu.

My discovery of this McChurch phenomenon set me on a course of What Ifs that changed everything. I pursued the answers to these questions like everything in my life depended on it, and the answers revealed who my Creator truly is and became this book. Even more unexpected, they revealed the truth of who I really am–the good, the bad, and the ugly–and freed me to worship on an infinitely deeper, more fulfilling level, free of fear for the first time. I discovered I could have spirituality *and* my religion. I could have comfort *and* freedom. I could be undamned *and* not have to grovel or apologize to anyone for being imperfect me and being undamned made me a much more effective, trustworthy, and forgiving spiritual emissary.

Everything I thought the Bible taught me was a lie. I overcame the lies in my life by piecing together this system and tools that worked for me and have worked for others to whom I have spoken.

This is a spiritual memoir that describes a system, an outlook and tools that made a huge alteration in my life. This is my truth and only my truth. While I deeply hope it helps others, I would never try to impose my truth or perceptions on anyone else. The events herein are true, described as I perceived them happening. As I healed and grew spiritually, some of my most important perceptions changed. To protect others' privacy, all names, places, and specific dates have been changed.

As I made this pilgrimage, here are some of the questions I kept asking of others and eventually answered for myself. The answers were surprising, but the questions themselves transformed me.

> What if we are all already who God created us to be, and all that is necessary is for us to be uncovered?

> What if everything we need to be "saved," forgiven, redeemed, transformed, and a source of inspiration and influence to others is *already* at our fingertips?

What if what some of us are being taught by our religion is the very thing that is holding us back from being all that God intends us to be?

What if some of us have been so traumatized by our religion that our very idea of faith is upside-down?

What if some of us are being taught things that are not true about the Bible and ourselves, that Jesus would never stand for, and those teachings are creating a lost tribe of disaffected believers?

What if the disaffected lost tribe has it right?

What if the answers we seek are far simpler and far more glorious than we can imagine?

What if my story of how I escaped this Old Testament Hell isn't just my story? What if there are millions of us?

What if the Bible isn't the whole story, but only the beginning of our story?

CHAPTER ONE

Jesus, Are You a Brand?

CHAPTER 1   *Jesus, Are You a Brand?*

Dear Jesus,
are you a brand?
Will you smite me where I stand
if I ask you to hold my hand?
A brand can't forgive
or teach me a better way to live
or love or show me the way.

Do these folks really speak for you
when they say, "Do as I say,
not as I do?"
They seem to
know my sins so well,
although I've never spoken of them.
Gossip is Gospel here, I hear.
But what is pure, and good and true –
the part that comes from you –
does not appear
to be marketable.
I'm not changing according to their timetable.
I'm too old for this, too young for that.
When I'm dead or delusional, will I fit?[2]

There are a growing number of us who are coming to realize that a number of stories being told today and attributed to Jesus don't have anything to do with what he said or came to do.[3]

My personal journey was a lesson learned the hard way. I was confronted with many things that didn't seem to add up. I stumbled on answers to questions I didn't know I had, and in searching for the answers, found a much deeper understanding of my Higher Power and myself. Some of these questions were:

> What happens when spirituality is approached in the same way as the mass production of hamburgers?
>
> Is salvation now a product? Are we congregants, or just consumers, or both?
>
> Is my personal spiritual relationship with God anywhere in this picture?

Why take it so personally? Because it is personal. Spiritual matters should be as intimate as the most treasured relationship, and yet, in some instances they are treated as anything but. Sometimes they are handled as big business. This was how I stumbled upon the McChurch.

It wasn't intentional. I was looking anywhere and everywhere for meaning and community, and I ran into the one-size-fits-all phenomenon.

Because I didn't completely fit the traditional Christian definition, I naturally gravitated toward those churches which reached out to the religious outcast, the disenfranchised, the skeptics, the atheists, those burned and branded by religion and those not already affiliated with a church.

I was looking for a place that celebrated the individual–the quirkiness that makes me unique. I thought I'd find a tribe of individuals who, like me, did not fit the traditional mold.

I found instead a fast-food chain with a steeple and a McDoctrine, and was burned and branded by an acute spiritual existentialism.

It had some surprising and insidious spiritual consequences, which I happily, and eventually, overcame. It also had some unexpected benefits. Mine is a cautionary tale, with a happy ending.

My encounters with McChurch were the catalyst that began the soul-searching, the spiritual and emotional excavation, and intense scrutiny of all things religious that resulted in my getting free.

The term "McChurch" does not refer to any particular size or denomination of church. I use "McChurch" to refer to a particular philosophical approach toward congregants. The approach is secular, like a corporate hierarchy. McChurches tend to tell their members who God wants them to be, without waiting to find out what they might have to say about it, and without letting God tell or show them what he might have to say about it.

Their approach is more like "What have you done for me lately?" and it says we are defined by our actions, not our hearts or motivations. The message can be we need to change and change fast to be on the right path, and by the way, there is only one path. But the hows and the whys of such change are not always defined well, or they are defined overly well and rigidly. The emphasis can be on the categorization of congregants according to what they've done in the past, or how they can best be used in filling the needs of the church itself, instead of on facilitating the gradual and unique blossoming, evolution, and fruition of each congregant's purpose and identity in God, and marveling in and celebrating this growth.

The focus is often on the business of the church, rather than igniting a desire in each of us to seek all God has in store for our lives and to equip us to GO CLAIM IT!

Instead of letting this process look different for each person, as God created each of us unique in our own way, McChurches tend to have only one version of the truth and a very limited number of options in finding it, like a fast-food restaurant menu. I experienced this sense of limitation and scarcity in what could have been an environment of miracles, and spoke to a number of other people who experienced the same thing.

At McChurch, I noticed and mourned the loss of the mystery, majesty, and the infinite facets of our creator that are the genesis of unforeseen possibilities and miracles. They were replaced by the limited and finite business of salvation. The pastors and theologians made room for those who excelled in creating and marketing brands for entities, products, and services. This is certainly intelligent and advantageous in many ways, but it can't help but have unintended consequences.

Before I finally found the perfect church fit for me, I

made quite a pilgrimage, sampling of all different kinds of churches. The events I describe happened, but they happened in more than one church, causing me to wonder how often they happened in others, and how many of us have similar stories. I'll be the first to admit I didn't have all the answers, but that was why I asked the questions.

The only way to recognize a McChurch is by paying attention to how you feel while attending. Does your personal truth suddenly seem untrue? Does it seem as if you are viewed more like a static object, like a photograph, capable of being "figured out" at first glance? Is there a sense of not being really seen or heard or known, and not much curiosity to see, hear or know the real you? Is there limitation and scarcity of spiritual opportunities?

Why Should We Care?
What do Kleenex, Martha Stewart, and McChurches have in common? All are brands. Today's church is not necessarily just a church. It can also be a franchise, a multi-national corporation, a brand, or perhaps even all three.

It was easy for me to be seduced by finally being part of the religious "in" crowd. It was cool how much the McChurch resembled the outside world. The music was frequently the same song selections I listened to on iTunes. The messages were really practical examples of how to live life. That made sense to me. I was used to being pursued as a consumer and filling out marketing surveys. It made sense to apply these corporate tools to church, and I still think it does.

But as I looked a little deeper, questions started to percolate on theological levels and on the basic humanity level. Would Jesus teach what these McChurches were teaching, or do these practices ignore or even, at times, hurt those whom Jesus valued most of all: the meek, poor in spirit, those who mourn and are in pain? Or are these people simply left behind?

The Mechanics of Marginalization

A brand is a symbol. It is a form of marketing shorthand. A brand can't do much. It is inanimate and inhuman. Its purpose is to attract buyers.

It can't forgive, redeem, or listen. It certainly cannot transform. People still can do these things, under the auspices of the brand, to the extent they don't run afoul of what the brand stands for.

Why is this important? The reason so many churches look like fast-food franchises is because in some ways they are and they have to be to attract the numbers to remain viable. Legally, a church is a "non-profit" entity for tax purposes, but business principles still apply. If there is more red than black on the balance sheet, programs will be discontinued, as will jobs. For this reason, every bit as much energy goes into the business and marketing plan for a church as does a fast-food franchise. Each church has to find its demographic niche and exploit it to the maximum possible. This isn't bad; it is reality.

What are the key components of any successful brand? Consistency and uniformity from store to store, restaurant to restaurant, package of pantyhose to package of pantyhose. There is a reason fast-food menus are so limited: consistency. There is a better chance to achieve consistency if there are only a few choices.

What is the McChurch translation of consistency? Conformity. Predictability. One Size Fits All. That can certainly be a Catch 22, when it comes to individual spiritual revelation and growth.

Here is the Church, Here is the Steeple. OMG, We've Forgotten the People!

Acceptance of one's unique personhood is the beginning of individual transformation. But how can this happen in the branded environment of a McChurch? What happens when the values of individuality of path are pitted against consistency and conformity within the organization?

There's something missing from this equation, and it is the individual. He or she has fallen through the cracks.

Repeatedly, the Bible speaks of spiritual transformation as a lifelong process, not an instant, recordable event that is here and then over. It must be an evolution, not a revolution, as this person walks closer and closer with God throughout his or her life.

God is not a squawk box taking our order in the drive-through lane.

Like a child who falls when learning to walk, a person growing in his or her spirituality will experience missteps and pain. Frequently, this pain is seen as undesirable in the church context because there is fear of frightening other congregants or because it looks like misbehaving. A person can actually be scolded and shamed for growing, confronting his or her mistakes, and wanting more. This can cause them to either stay silent in their pain or victimhood, or regress to the point of self-loathing.

If no one knows us as we really are, we run the risk of becoming victims of self-hatred. If we can be loved by somebody, anybody, who sees us as we really are, we can then begin to accept ourselves and transform. But this process is a long movie, not a single picture.

The McChurch model of transformation today does not mirror the individual's process or even take it into account. It does not mirror or even take into account God's timeframe. There is often no room for individuality or stumbles, because frequently a corporate marketing timetable is superimposed on personal spiritual transformation.

As non-denominational mega-churches get larger and larger, our imagination and discernment of God can get narrower and narrower. Our attention is diverted from the infinite, incomprehensible nature of God to the many looming concerns of running the church and keeping it running.

Transformation occurs from surrender, acceptance of self and others, and unconditional love. But, to be unconditionally accepted and loved, one has to be recognized, seen, and respected as an individual.

Our lessons, our trials, and our tears are written out of the scene in McChurches, because transformation cannot be predicted, forecast, or managed in advance. There is nothing predictable or consistent about personal journeys.

We Have a New Dictionary
A brand is nothing but a label itself. The label stands for the

things we want consumers to think of when they think of our church, product, or service. A brand can't recognize you and love you for who you are, or who you are trying to be. *You don't get points for trying to transform, you only get points for transforming immediately.*

In the past, the corporation had one definition, the non-profit corporation had another definition, and the Church had yet another, separate definition. Now, not only is there overlap, to a certain extent the definitions, goals, and missions may be identical and interchangeable.

What is new in the mix is the extreme level of competition from church to church to attract new followers and grow at a time when the numbers of those who define themselves as regular church attendees have been steadily declining.

But one steadily growing demographic is the "Seekers," people who are on the fence about all of this. They are the generation raised essentially without a church or a theology.

It is a challenge to grab and hold the attention of a generation used to surfing hundreds of channels of cable TV while they simultaneously Facebook and text their friends. Their standard is influenced to a large extent by entertainment value, and where they go, McChurch will follow.

This trend can give rise to intense competition among members to be seen, recognized, and accepted within a McChurch, because the most extreme and dramatic stories are honestly more entertaining. Unwittingly, and with the best of intentions, people and their stories may be labeled as "sermon-worthy" or not and someone who has been quietly walking the right path for many years may not make the cut. This weeding-out process is necessary. There is only so much time in a 50-minute service. All of this comes from the best of intentions: to reach and reach out to the greatest number of people.

The Destruction of Grace

All of these secular pressures can result in formulas and rules in the McChurch that mimic those of the Old Testament Pharisees, the teachers who tried to use their rules to trap Jesus.

> Where is my Jesus in all of this?
>
> Is God limited by the Sunday morning production schedule?
>
> If Jesus walked into the Church of the Immaculate Hamburger, would he make a whip and start flailing it at people like he did with the moneychangers, or would "Security" see him coming in the parking lot and usher him out?
>
> What if there is no room for you in your religion?
>
> Is there still grace at McChurch?
>
>> What did Jesus think of the law of continuity and survival of the fittest?
>> ~ He didn't give a damn.
>>
>> How did Jesus respond to those in pain and in sin?
>> ~With grace.

Who or what was Jesus about, the organization or the individual?

It appears to many of us today that Christians have come to represent many of the things Jesus came to free us from, as Rob Bell points out in *Jesus Wants to Save Christians, A Manifesto for the Church in Exhile*.[4] When he happened upon the woman caught in the act of adultery, who faced stoning by her accusers, Jesus did not condemn or even criticize her. He challenged her attackers to look at their own moral track records.

He didn't join them or conform to the mob mentality. He admonished them, saying those without sin could throw their rocks. Jesus encouraged her to sin no more, but he saw her, recognized her, loved her, and accepted her.

He didn't reduce her to a label.

He called the religious leaders of his day *whitewashed tombs*.[5] He taught us to be who we are, not who we want or ought to be. When asked by the rich man how to enter the Kingdom of heaven, he replied, "Sell your possessions and … follow me."[6]

Not mainstream.

Not consistent.

Not conformist.

Jesus worked on the Sabbath. He hung out with prostitutes, misfits, and tax collectors.

He, like all the prophets before him, cared nothing for "toeing the line" or fitting in.

How about the people Jesus picked to be his reps and found

CHAPTER 1 🌱 *Jesus, Are You a Brand?*

the church? Were they the top one percent?

Peter, who later founded Christ's church, was a screw-up. He was not cable-ready and never really mastered the sound bite. By all accounts, Peter did not start out as an inspiring leader. He wasn't loyal. He put his foot in his mouth. He denied Christ three times.

But, during this time, he was incubating the abilities that would allow him to go out and found the Church. No one could see it but God. Because Peter repeatedly experienced God's compassion, forgiveness, and grace in the person of Christ, he could preach about forgiveness, compassion, and the love of our Savior with conviction.

And we all know about Paul... the Christian killer.

So, where are the modern-day prophets? How would they survive at McChurch?

In a culture of conformity, where can the Truth tellers reside? Are they now irrelevant, in a world of talking points, sound bites, and branded people or do we need them more than ever?

These questions have been asked before, and today's modern churches were an attempt to embrace the people standing on the sidelines.

Welcome to the land of unintended consequences.

No formula can work because faith isn't a formula, salvation isn't an equation, and people, like their God, cannot be defined.

Simple.

For my thoughts are not your thoughts, neither are your ways my ways.[7]

In *How (Not) to Speak of God*, Peter Rollins compares God to a painting that speaks to us in different ways at different times, thus making it necessary to return to the painting again and again.[8]

This is such a beautiful and perfect analogy. It speaks of more than God's infinite nature. It speaks of his changeable and limber nature, not capable of being confined or defined by any of us, ever. Each of us can only describe our individual, unique, and personal encounters with our God. Generalizations don't apply. They miss the mark. Consistency be damned.

For we are God's handiwork, created in Christ Jesus to do good works, which God prepared in advance for us to do.[9] Labeling God's handiwork isn't Biblical, is it?

As I understand it, *theology* means a discourse or talk about God. If that is what it means, then we are all theologians, aren't we?

Each and every one of us has quite a lot to say, all of it unique, sacred, and valuable. Every tear, every struggle, every setback has set us on the path to be able to encourage another, and, as such, is as sacred as any temple.

I didn't know this fundamental truth. I put all of my faith in people with feet of clay, just like me. Mine is a cautionary tale of what happens when someone has way too much faith in "experts" and far too little in God and herself.

But this is also a chronicle of how I woke up, wised up, and freed myself.

I have no particular axe to grind. I go to church still and love my church like family. I have wonderful associations with many churches in my city, and get something unique and significant from each one. I would not part with any of them.

There was a lot of trial and error, though, before I could feel at home at McChurch or any other place of worship. What follows is how I arrived at this spiritual destination.

CHAPTER TWO

The Church of the Immaculate Hamburger

There are no discipleship factories.
~ Dave Haney

CHAPTER 2 🍔 *The Church of the Immaculate Hamburger*

Dear Jesus,
I feel less than special.
I feel less than marginal.
How can anyone love me here?
How can you even find me here?
Why do I feel that way here?
Are you here?
The uniforms are missing,
but the menu is the same
no matter the location.
They say they love me
but I don't know.
This brand of love
makes me feel cold.
If you made me unique,
why does this place make me feel
like customer number 5,000,000?
Please forgive me,
I did not know
I was seeking redemption at Burger King®
Salvation to go,
with a side of fries, thanks.
I will pay at the drive-thru window,
tailor my requests to the pre-fab menu
and go.[10]

Where Is The Why?

At the worst time of my life, I went looking for what was missing. I looked and searched and looked some more and what I found was a series of soul-stripping experiences so similar in a succession of churches I came to recognize and describe in this chapter as the Church of the Immaculate Hamburger. I too, had my brush with McChurch. I felt spiritually dead. I went in search of purpose and, lo and behold, I walked into the Church of the Immaculate Hamburger.

This seemed to be the place where I could take a quick spiritual refresher course and get back on track.

I had no idea who I was spiritually, or in any other sense, but I thought I did. All it would take would be to ask the pastor or pastors what I was doing wrong and correct it.

I had always thought I had the answers. I grew up in the church and was raised on the scriptures. I knew the Ten Commandments and even tried to keep them. I thought that made me spiritually mature and a truth-seeker. That wasn't true.

The truth is I was barely formed, spiritually. I had no idea of how broken I was, or even in what ways.

This intersection of my spiritual and emotional pain and the Church of the Immaculate Hamburger eventually broke me open and began my healing and transformation. But, at the time, it seemed like anything but a beginning.

What I thought I was looking for was spiritual wisdom and guidance and discernment. I wanted to know why God didn't seem to like me and what I should do to get him to. I knew

CHAPTER 2 🐿 *The Church of the Immaculate Hamburger*

I had done something wrong, but I wasn't sure where I fell off the beam. Surely someone could set me straight so I could begin to do a better job of managing my life.

I now realize I was searching for grace– something I had undoubtedly experienced at some point in my life but for some reason couldn't recognize or express then. I did find a lot of people on fire for the Lord and earnestly trying to help, but it never hit the mark. The answers and advice seemed too general to make sense.

When I was in my spiritual meltdown and wavering between suicide and atheism, I was told a lot of interesting and important things. I was told, "Go talk to that person over there and they will minister to you." That person over there did attempt to minister to me by relating his own personal experience and spiritual journey, which, most often, had nothing to do with me or my journey. It was like I wasn't in the room.

After these encounters, the other person seemed to be visibly relieved and lightened after sharing his or her story, and to be sure, many stories were inspirational and inspired admiration, but I left these conversations feeling even more isolated and alone than before. I began to believe there truly was no one who could relate to or understand me.

At that time, I thought I was damned.

I was making a lot of new friends but none knew me– really. As if speaking to a toddler, they would ask, "You do know all of this isn't really about you, right?" I gleaned from the question I was on the wrong track, but it gave me not the slightest hint of what the right track would even look like.

I received recitations of scripture and got lots of advice. Of course, it was my fault for asking; I asked for way too much advice. Lots and lots of people in 3- or 4-year marriages advised me on my 20-year marriage. Of course, I now know a 20-year marriage breeds humility, so no one with a long-term marriage felt comfortable telling me how to run mine. It didn't stop me from asking them, though.

The fact that all of these people were willing to give of their time to meet with me is a blessing, and I made many good friends through this process who are still my friends to this day.

This is my whole point: These people were not being malicious. They were doing the best they could with the tools and information they had at the time. Just as I was doing the best I could with the tools and information I had at the time.

But it wasn't enough. Admittedly, I was light-years away from true spirituality and didn't know it. I had a huge part in not getting where I needed to be, because I didn't want to see my life as it truly was. That would have meant I had failed spectacularly, and failure and shame were what I feared most.

Finally, I began to question the truth of something offered at face value.

I began to ask questions of my church and myself.

With that, I began my journey.

I asked myself what was missing from these unsatisfying encounters, and it was the "Why?" Not a single person asked me "Why?" Not a single question was asked of me concerning my motivations or heart. The most important aspect of my spiritual crisis and search–the context–was absent.

The interpretation my brain came up with for this dilemma was that my situation had nothing to do with me whatsoever. I remember thinking how bizarre that was and wondering if I should exit and never return.

The apparent randomness of it all had me hooked. I kept trying to earn my way in; I wanted to have the answers, and I hoped they would rub off on me with frequent church attendance. What I wanted and needed to heal spiritually and be reconciled to God didn't happen. It wasn't even on the agenda. However, part of the reason it didn't happen was because I didn't ask myself what I needed spiritually. My heart knew the truth, but my mind was on a completely different track.

I now know what I was looking for was unconditional love and acceptance from my faith community. What I wanted and needed was for someone to see me as I truly am—a broken tangle of emotions and fears, but still striving to progress, learn, and heal—and love me anyway... like God does.

Since I didn't know what it looked like, I had to be shown. Until I was convinced I was loved and accepted, even though hugely flawed, I could not do anything but judge, resent, and fear my fellow man. It wasn't in me to give that which I had no concept of.

I didn't need someone to check up on me by inquiring what I was doing. I needed someone to ask how I was doing, what I was feeling, and most importantly, why.

I wanted to talk about the Bible. I loved to talk about God and the Bible, but I wanted it to relate to me and my life and my circumstances. I wanted to know what my specific lesson was.

The Cosmic View

> *What we see Jesus doing again and again—in the midst of constant reminders about the seriousness of following him, living like him, and trusting him—is widening the scope and expanse of his saving work...*
>
> *Whatever categories have been created, whatever biases are hanging like a mist in the air, whatever labels and assumptions have gone unchecked and untested, he continually defies, destroys, and disregards.*[11]

I believe everything else flows from the ability to see the context of each individual's life and how it makes their walk and experience unique and even sacred. I believe it is impossible to get to know the heart of a person without the "why," and it is impossible to offer unconditional acceptance and love to anyone without understanding their "why." Without understanding how the person and their experience is a completely one of a kind replica of God, I can't do anything the Bible tells us we are to be doing.

If God is infinite in his characteristics and capacity, then there must be an infinite number of ways to mirror God, and there must be an infinite number of lessons and paths to follow, all unique.

All sacred.

Without the key ingredient of context, the "why," I can only put people in prefab boxes, judge them and cast them out, or even worse, use them as a vessel for me to project my pain,

experience, and arrogance onto. But if I do that, I have negated:
> Grace
>> Salvation
>>> Second Chances
>>>> The New Testament

The ways to transformation are infinite. But, the Church of the Immaculate Hamburger is about a product, consistent from location to location and day to day.

Grace comes from the heart, not the mind. Grace is the byproduct of compassion, acceptance, and unconditional love. All of these things well up from the heart, not the mind.

These things happen in a certain order:

First, a hurting person feels genuine love and acceptance from others. Then she begins to feel it for herself and toward herself. Learning to love herself, she dares to believe God might love her, too. This transforms her. Her mind and heart renew, and she begins to truly love and accept others, helping them to transform.

The "Why" is key because asking it in a non-condemning manner in a safe environment leads people to unmask their wounds, to unburden what is troubling them, hiding them, and holding them back. It gives the wounded the courage to be transparent and transformative. For me, it was the catalyst that started the entire chain reaction of healing, grace, acceptance, and transformation.

Where Is The Love?

> *Above all else, guard your heart, for everything you do flows from it.*[12]

If God created us to be totally unique, then each of us has our own path and our own timetable. None of us is ugly, and our behavior cannot be judged as ugly until the full context is revealed.

It is incremental. One area is healed at a time. Why censure non-conformity? What if God is telling a person who has been used by others her whole life to say "No" for once, to not conform? And then she gets to church, where she is pressured to conform. The context of her life, as she sees it, is to not conform.

If her church doesn't back her up, will she have to choose between submission to the goals of the church and surrender to God? Will her confidence and trust in God succumb to fear of consequences? Will she get compassion or legalism? What she gets has influence on whom she becomes. Will anxiety stifle her authenticity, the authenticity necessary to heal? Will she be given authority over her own life and allowed to believe she is hearing from God, or will she be undermined? Will she be transformed into a vessel of light, or will she hide what is strange and unique about her, trapped in an adolescence of the heart and mind?

Really, no matter what we believe, all a faith community can do for its members is to love them like family, and to work to see them as God does. Everything else stems from this. Isn't the failure to do so limiting God, making him small, and reducing the teachings of Jesus to bumper stickers?

Evolution Not Revolution

Learning is movement from moment to moment.
     J. Krishnamurti

When I experienced and learned to recognize grace and acceptance, my transformation began. But it was a process, not an event. It happened when God had prepared me sufficiently to face what I needed to face. Not a second before. What The Church of the Immaculate Hamburger thought or even I thought of the timeframe was irrelevant.

My mind and my heart had been renewed and strengthened as I found a loving and safe haven to see my destructive patterns and myself. All of the sharp talk, scripture, and advice, however well intended, did nothing but drive me deeper into hiding and put me in defense mode. I couldn't grow from a defensive posture.

What Would Jesus Order at The Church of The Immaculate Hamburger?

He just might have ordered the McPreachers out of the temple. I don't think he meant for us to check our brains at the door and slavishly worship the trappings of religion instead of him. My guess is he would be appalled at the one-size-fits-all approach. I think everything in the Bible's New Testament written about Jesus, and particularly the words attributed to him, indicate he was about loving and accepting the individuals who came into his path, and about transforming them through grace.

He was about acceptance and love, and seeing the individual as God saw them because he was God. He employed the genius of parables to drive his points home.

The parables were specific examples of how certain people behaved in certain circumstances. They were about people. Individuals. They were told and retold in such a way that it is impossible to generalize, dummy down, or mass-produce them. They were designed to protect us from our worst tendencies and ourselves.

Some of us, including me, function best with as little ambiguity as possible. Rules motivate us and give us structure. Guilt motivates us when we break them. Rules give me a way to gauge myself versus other people. "I'm not that bad." Codependents like me, finding no rules stringent enough to whip ourselves with, will invent them. It's a way of feeling superior and inferior all at the same time.

The whole point of parables is we don't know and we can't. The Bible is the sacred word of God, but since we aren't God, there is a large chance that we will misunderstand. In the parables, each person and each story stands on its own.

Each is a sacred story, like each of us.

So, what would Jesus think of making our very souls the subject of exhaustive market research? What would Jesus think of the reducing of people to commodities, assets, and liabilities? Those people are the church. There is no church without them.

So many of us began with an authentic encounter with God, only to have it reduced to nothing but doctrine. For many, this ends or warps our faith before it has the opportunity to take root. An image or description of God isn't God.[13]

I do this all of the time. I discount and denigrate the living, breathing child of God before me, even the child in the mirror, for an interpretation of what I think God is saying, subjective to my own shortcomings and wounds. I let other people do this, too. I let them tell me my truth, and I believe it.

If this is true, it means God knows me better than any man or woman on earth, including myself.

It also means he alone has authority over my life and its meaning and purpose. That means every life is essential and sacred because it is designed by God and designed to enlighten and transform others. And that means every emotion, challenge, experience we have is sacred as any temple, no matter how it may look on the outside. God has the long view and the endgame in mind. What mortal can say otherwise?

This means a host of joyous things! It means when a person appears to be acting out, or regressing in their faith, they may be progressing and doing exactly what God wants them to do. This is precisely what the context of my spiritual journey was. I believed it but could not make anyone else believe it.

It is entirely possible the very behavior the one-size-fits-all church thought so deplorable was causing God to rejoice! Now, with the benefit of 20/20 hindsight, I can see that was probably the case. God could see it, of course, but no one else could, and the very thing that caused me to seek, pursue, and find God was hurt feelings about being misunderstood.

How can you know where someone is going, if you don't know where he or she has come from? If what I see is only according to the angle and the light, and my vision is always compromised, then why would I criticize?

Who can predict what will be the transformational catalysts in another person's life? We are all living parables to show and illustrate the wonderful and sacred variety of personhood, and to show in our lives that any experience, any emotion, and any tragedy can lead any person to divine transformation.

CHAPTER THREE

My Story: Part One
Extreme Spiritual Makeover
or
How to Lose Yourself Without Really Trying

*For here we are not afraid to follow the truth
wherever it may lead.*
~ Thomas Jefferson

Snapshot #1:

Sometime in the late 1960s, in a large house on a quiet suburban street. Viewed from the street, it was a square mustard yellow box, with asbestos siding protecting its inhabitants from view. The front yard was a perfectly edged, green square. It sat next to a canary yellow box and a beige box. Inside, it was anything but quiet.

Every Saturday the husbands would emerge from their boxes and participate in the ritual and spectacle of yard work. It began after breakfast and was an all day affair.

There were three of us kids and I was the eldest and only girl. The canary yellow house next door housed a perfectly matched set of kids: a girl my age, a boy my middle brother's age and a girl my youngest brother's age. Our younger siblings got to buy clothes off the wrack, while the eldest girls had to deal with our mothers' attempts to master Simplicity Patterns, and wore- home made clothes. We had a pair of school shoes and a pair of patent-leather church shoes and that was it.

Our moms took art classes together, frosted each other's hair, and had an annual "Thank God!" Bloody Mary party on the first day of school. We went to church most Sundays, because that is what people did. I got confirmed in the church on my 13th birthday, along with almost all of my friends from school.

Dinner was at 6pm. Period. Attendance was mandatory and there were no excuses. Both of my brothers played Varsity football, and the whole family attended their games.

We watched TV together as a family every night and

everyone went to bed at 10PM. Period. My family always watched the Ed Sullivan show together, and then, one night, there they were. The Supremes.

The music went straight into my soul and made it shimmer. I wanted to give that experience to everyone I could. God had given me my first tool to return my world to sanity, no matter what was happening around me.

The Supremes were the first thing I ever wanted to be.

I heard the beautiful harmonies. I saw the graceful choreographed arm motions. I memorized the glamorous gowns, wigs, and makeup, and my only thought was, "I could do this. I have to do this." They were so beautiful and confident. The Motown beat was infectious and vibrantly alive.

The memory of that desire and dream is as vivid in my gut and heart today as the day it first formed.

When I heard the beautiful words to "Ain't No Mountain High Enough," that was it. There couldn't be another song as magnificent. I wanted to dance the first time I heard them and every time thereafter. I would stop what I was doing when their song was on the radio and dance, pretending I was one of them. They had the trifecta: soul, glamour, and insane talent. I loved the beat of their songs. It was happy and you could feel it in your body. There was no need to count it out like a march. I remember watching them perform on television in the oak-paneled family room with my family and watching my parents—my mom's legs were crossed but that top foot swung up and down with the rhythm and my dad's feet tapped.

I would stand in the bathtub singing, with the shower

curtain wrapped around me like it was one of those gorgeous evening gowns. My radio was blaring through every waking moment and saw me through every crisis and heartbreak until I reached college. At some point I told this dream to my family, who, naturally, thought it was funny. In jest someone commented, "Well, you might as well go join the circus."

I didn't understand the comment, but I took it to heart. It felt like I had made some kind of mistake, and I resolved to correct it, taking my first step to approval junky-dom. It wasn't a big step. It wasn't like falling off of a cliff. It was small. A small note of correction I placed in my brain to refer to again.

Snapshot # 2
Sometime in the 1990s. In a suburban house on a wide street lined with large, old oak trees, I lie with my eyes open wide, mind turning in circles. It is in the early, early morning hours. I can hear the cicadas chirping and an owl calling in the back yard. They sound so loud I can't possibly sleep. Down the hall, my daughter is snoring. My husband snores and tosses a little next to me. My son sleeps quietly. This has become very typical. I lie vigilant each night waiting for and expecting I know not what. I feel anxious, as if the bottom is about to drop out of our lives.

How did I get from there to here? Slowly, but surely. One note of correction, one decision based on fear at a time, until this was what my life was like:

Morning Routine
I sit down with a cup of coffee where I won't be disturbed.

57 UNDAMNED

I stare out the window at the sunshine and trees and let the negative thoughts pour in. Every time my thought shifts to something higher, I return it to what is wrong.

I dwell upon and grieve the past. I review and mentally correct all of the mistakes I have made, going back to childhood. I think about all of the missed opportunities and wasted time. I ponder all the times I was mistreated and attempt to decipher the cause.

I think about my body and wonder if my age isn't beginning to show, focusing on random aches and pains to confirm this notion.

I worry about finances and let the fear take hold. If they are going well now, I tell myself disaster is inevitable and probably on the way.[14]

This was how I lived my life until I freed myself. I was the biggest sinner in the world, alive or dead, I was sure of it. So was everyone else I knew or trusted, or so I believed. I was surer of this and had more faith in this conviction than in God himself. No one can ever accuse me of getting things right the first time around. God has been giving me the same lesson over and over since I can remember.

But I am not a queen of subtlety or reading tealeaves. I am not always self-aware. It has usually taken a spiritual occurrence on par with a grand piano landing on my head to produce a spiritual awakening.

While the young girl and the woman in the snapshots had many differences, they had one thing in common: a love of words. They go straight through to my heart. They have been both my gift and my downfall. I love to craft them in a poem, lyric, or phrase, and I respect and admire this ability in others. I love the power of words to capture, influence, and inspire. They can be magical and miraculous. They have a rhythm, drive, and energy that are music to me.

Somewhere around age 10 or 11, I began to use my love for words as therapy for what was going on in my life. I wrote poetry to make sense of the things happening in my life over which I had no control. It was an emotional outlet and made things look and sound beautiful and elegant. The rhymes and meter of the poems gave me structure and logic to superimpose on my situation.

We moved to a new house in an affluent neighborhood, boasting the best school district in town. My parents wanted us in this school and bought a house they could barely afford. It was a fixer-upper, owned by a family with a pet monkey they kept indoors. There was a home-made fountain in the back yard made from a copper kettle, stocked with trout and blue gills the family caught fishing.

When we moved in, there were liquor bottles in the oven, under the carpets, and on the curtain rods. Despite the fact that our house was a "bargain," there were signs we didn't have the balance sheet to carry it off well yet. My mom made my dresses, and I had only two pairs of shoes. At the time, this was nothing unusual. But I began to hear my parents talk about the "country club set" a lot and the fact that we were not part of it. I would hear the phrase over and over, "We are not the Rockefellers."

UNDAMNED

Being rich was somehow bad. I made another mental note.

The school was as good as people said, and I adjusted to being the new kid. The children were friendly and the teachers were interested and involved.

My next door neighbor, Amy, and I were in the same 5th grade class. There were several kids our ages in almost every house on our block and we all went to the same school. We were all ordered by our mothers to not set foot inside our houses until dinnertime. We had no choice but to get along and play with each other. Our parents trusted us, and we had the run of the neighborhood and well beyond, as long as we were home by dinner. We never had to ask permission or give an itinerary. Adventure was wherever our feet or bikes could take us.

Our house was full of laughing kids, putting on skits imitating television shows. Our front yard was where everyone wanted to be. We had neighborhood baseball, basketball, and tackle football games almost every evening of the week. My parents were the "cool" ones, though I'm not sure why.

But I became aware my parents had feet of clay. There were financial pressures and fighting. I had never heard my parents fight in any of our previous houses, but in this house, the sound reverberated off the walls and carried upstairs. Every evening, my brothers and I were banished to upstairs or outdoors for one hour while my parents had "grownup hour." They had cocktails and talked about their day. My brothers and I sat on the stairs and listened to them argue and tried to figure out which way our lives were headed.

This was normal for us, so we just went with it. We just thought this was part of how my parents loved each other. There were a lot of words flying around, some of them angry and hurtful. Sometimes, there were pork chops flying around at the dinner table. There was an undercurrent of something in our house I now know was the anger and frustration carried by two people who loved each other but were not compatible in any way, but I couldn't put a finger on it then. Both parents loved us so much they stayed together for the kids. So much hope and happiness deferred with the best of intentions.

Up until I was around age 11, the words of the Bible were not harsh or scary. They were gorgeous and made me feel warm and safe. I would turn to my children's Bible in the privacy and secrecy of my room if I needed comfort, strength, or guidance. I knew instinctively if I was confused, God was a good place to start.

But then the angry undercurrent in my house bled into my children's Bible. The words became scary, condemning, and judgmental. They became a list of "should nots" that gradually formed the parameters of my life. It never occurred to me these words were outside of me and couldn't make me do or believe anything. It never occurred to me to ask myself if they were true. They just were.

I wanted to be right. I wanted to never make a mistake that would cause my parents to argue. I believed the words of the Bible would help me get there, if I could follow them perfectly.

Because I loved words, and was very susceptible to them, I gave them the power to give me spiritual life or death in and of themselves, without question. I was allowed to live only in that very narrow space between those words. I don't know where I got that idea, but it became my constant truth. The words in the Bible became the altar at which I prostrated myself every day.

It was a very gradual, subtle, elegant kind of spiritual suicide.

Because I wanted to belong, I gauged myself by others' words. I gave others the power to exhort and inspire, or to lessen, cheapen, and damn.

From my fourteenth birthday until I reached 20, I left personhood and began to see myself as a commodity, a religious product.

I thought I was living a blameless life. What I didn't pay any attention to were my internal and very damning interpretations of these words I used to guide my behavior. It was just a few Bible verses in the books of Corinthians, Ephesians, and Exodus that sent me on my way to self-damnation.

I certainly was not motivated to commit spiritual suicide. But this is exactly what I did using three key scriptures. I lived in a cage of my own making for half a century, and I believed the Bible told me to do so.

I used them to judge and enslave myself, and to judge and separate myself from others. I latched onto them and worshipped them as static and immutable – while God was standing on his head to show me that he was the exact opposite.

The peculiar thing is, the Scriptures themselves are pretty innocuous, but when read together, they became a cage with lead walls, buried at the bottom of the earth.

God didn't tell me to read them together or ignore the very different contexts of each passage. I put them together because I was doing a Biblical search on how to love somebody romantically and not get sent to Hell. So, even though the first provision is not necessarily referring to romantic love, but more about love of mankind, I interpreted it as an edict about romantic relationships. Like a masochistic and Victorian version of *Cosmo*.

Here they are:

> *Love is patient and kind... love does not insist on its own way... it does not boast, it is not proud... it is not easily angered, it keeps no record of wrongs... It always protects, always trusts, always hopes, and always perseveres. Love never fails.*[15]

> *Wives, submit yourselves to your own husbands as you do to the Lord.*[16]

> *You shall not commit adultery.*[17]

Wall #1 of the cage

My translation of the first scripture: Love means there is no me. Anger is a sin and so is meeting my own needs. Therefore, having a self is selfish. I must not fail.

Wall #2 of the cage

My translation of the second scripture: If I sleep with someone, it is a death sentence. I am married to that person and there is no escape except death. Relationships are static, permanent, and cannot be negotiated.

Wall # 3 of the cage

My translation of the third scripture: Don't ever violate scriptures 1 or 2 – or else.

As an added bonus I found a fourth Scripture to create wall #4 of the cage, Leviticus 20:10: *If a man commits adultery with another man's wife–with the wife of his neighbor–both the adulterer and the adulteress must be put to death.*

My translation: No way out. No hope. No escape.

Instead of expanding my life and opening me to others, worshipping these words caused me to make every decision based on fear, shame, or fear of being shamed. According to my personal translation of the Scriptures, loving anyone was bad if it could remotely lead to sex, and loving anyone was a permanent state. It was an either/or proposition. Have God in my life and be a nun, or have normal sexuality and have no God.

Imagine facing adolescence with this mindset! Imagine trying to negotiate a love relationship with this attitude. I was entering into a world without protective boundaries because I believed having a self was selfish. I wasn't giving myself a chance in Hell. (Or maybe I was.)

With this belief system in place, the world was full of danger. Things that should have been fun and full of growth opportunities, like dating, were terrifying. God was up there with his finger on the Smite button, ready to push it if I stepped out of line.

When I was fourteen, I started dating. I had these scriptures and my mother's words about virginity in my head at all times. At that age, kids couldn't drive so there was a great deal of supervision. Dating was safe, fun, and no big deal. But I barely had a handful of these dates before I met my first love. Let's call him Bill. A boyfriend was the perfect catalyst to cause spiritual and emotional torment, and put my religious convictions to the test.

We started dating when I turned fifteen and we were sophomores in high school. I don't know how he did it, but all of our dates were alone, with him driving. I didn't question it at the time. My guess is he was older than he let on.

Being a good Christian girl who was taught the Ten Commandments, I was determined to stay a virgin. But I was madly in love by our fourth date and stayed that way for ten years.

I was still reading the Bible every day at this point. Becaue I was in love, I let 1st Corinthians 13:1-7 and its definition of love dictate my life:

> *If I have faith that can move mountains but have not love, I am nothing. If I speak in the tongues of men and angels but have not love, I am a clanging gong... Love is not self-seeking, is not easily angered and keeps no record of wrongs. It always protects, always hopes, always perseveres. Love never fails.*

Nail One in My Spiritual Coffin

What I heard in my head was: I'm worthless if no one loves me. Failing in love is not an option, and there's no way out or any other option.

I had no concept of shades of gray. The King James Version of the Bible we read as children was even more severe. I interpreted the following portion as a Universal Unalterable Truth:

> *Love suffers all things. Forgives all things. Bears all things. Seeks not its own way.*[18]

This was the pivotal point in my spiritual and emotional formation, and I had it wrong. What a difference context would have made. This became my default decision-maker: *Suffering was part of the equation.*

I took the Bible at face value without questioning its relevance to my particular life in any way. If it was the word of God, as I had been taught, it was not to be questioned. It said I didn't have the right to get my own way. It said suffering in love is expected, and my only alternative was to forgive. According to my interpretation, I had to sit there and take it. I believed God wanted me to.

In my family and in the families of my closest friends, we were taught our word was our bond and breaking a promise or commitment was the same thing as deliberately lying. Lying was a sin, according to the Ten Commandments, my preacher, and my dad. *Thou shalt not bear false witness.*[19] I heard sermons about "getting it right before it's too late." I thought people who broke the Ten Commandments were going to Hell.

Therefore, if I loved someone, I believed I had to stick with them, even if my health, welfare, and very life hung in the balance. My credo was so logical, in its twisted way, like a math proof of damnation.

These scriptures book-ended my life and perceptions of love, foreclosing choices I otherwise could have made, options I otherwise could have seen, and joy I otherwise could have had.

This mindset caused me to attract abuse and manipulation because I never did anything about it. It also had a huge role in every decision I made, and often kept me from making decisions in my own best interest.

On our first date, Bill and I went to get pizza and he drank beer. I didn't want any because I wanted to never drink, I was a health nut, and we were under age. He made an issue of it, but I won that round. However, he clearly disapproved.

At the end of our date, I said the obligatory "Thanks, I had a great time!" and kissed him goodnight. His response was, "Yeah, right."

I was pretty well convinced I would never see him again, and that hurt because I thought he was great. That I concluded he was great after this date might have indicated my perceptions were a little off, if I had been paying attention.

There actually was a second date at the same place and I was given the same "dare." I tried to refuse, weakly. And his response was, "Why do you have to be so frigid? You're such a goody-two shoes. That's boring. Why don't you at least try it?"

He won that round and every round after. I wouldn't even stand up for myself. It didn't occur to me to do so. I was being polite and not making waves.

There was alcohol present every time we got together for the next ten years. Even during lunch at school. At least twice a week we would go out to lunch, drink margaritas, and come back late to class. I would walk in wobbly and late, and the teachers let it go because I was in the top twenty students, and could handle my work. This was also before the Dram Shop lawsuits and laws were enacted, and before MADD.[20]

In the space of two weeks, I compromised one of my core beliefs for love. Not even for love; for like. Not a single person commented, since I was "performing" as I should. I was on the honor roll. I never really caused any trouble for anyone.

Since others' words ruled my life, I assumed everything was okay and forged ahead with redoubled gusto. This was my personality. Serious. Dutiful. People-pleasing. No one made me that way but me. But religion helped me elevate people-pleasing and neuroses to an art form.

Now I can see that my one and only was a raging alcoholic in the making, but all I saw at the time was his disapproval, and that was enough.

My parents were going through their own drama during this time, as their marriage had begun the process of disintegration. They had to know I was coming in drunk from my dates, but I got good grades and functioned highly, so it was never mentioned. There were also two younger brothers to deal with.

School was something at which I naturally excelled. It was

all about the rules. It was about listening to others' words and following them to the letter. I could do that! I could be what the situation required. Naturally very competitive because I was a perfectionist, I couldn't fail or make a mistake and still be someone I liked. Someone might have critical words for or about me if I failed.

Our high school was considered a prep school, breeding much competition and ambition. I let others copy my answers and thought nothing of it. I was being "loving." Bill was in my math class and I let him copy my work every single day for that year. Even though I had done the work, staying up late studying and figuring out the answers, frequently after a date with him, I never thought he was stealing something I had earned and was mine, not his. After all, "Love bears all things, gives all things, forgives all things…" etc., etc.

I was learning a really warped concept of love, and I thought the Bible was the basis. I may have been a kid, but it was not lost on me that the few women mentioned in the Bible were models of submission. This made a huge impression and influenced how I saw and related to men, particularly authority figures for most of my life. It also impacted my spirituality in countless, unpredictable ways that would only reveal themselves much later on.

During my high school years, my mom periodically would talk to me about my virginity. What she wanted to impart to me was my virginity was the highest gift I could give anyone. Logically, I had trouble with the concept that my hymen was more treasured than my mind or my heart, but I was a good girl and afraid of going to Hell, so I endeavored to stay pure.

Like most of my peers, I failed. This ended up being a festering source of guilt through most of my life. Now, as an adult, I recognize she wasn't saying my hymen was worth more than my mind and soul. She understood wherever my body went my heart and soul would follow. In retrospect, I should have listened more closely.

By my junior year of high school, God was still in my life, but I was in my life less and less. I had begun the process of checking out and refusing to take responsibility for protecting myself, respecting myself, and getting and keeping good things in my life, because God was going to do that if I behaved and was perfect. If I didn't behave, I would be punished and I would deserve it. That was the contract, and I believed the Bible told me so. It was totally out of my hands. In my conscious mind my soul was everything, but unconsciously I was behaving as if it meant nothing.

Despite my best efforts, I was a teenager in love, with cascading hormones and a worshipful adoration of my hormone-addled boyfriend. The most momentous decision in my life at this point wasn't even a decision.

Boyfriend and I were "parking" and messing around and things got particularly urgent. I started to pull back rather than plummet over the edge, but Bill became irate and impatient. He had one of those Tall Boy beers and demanded I drink it or he would break up with me. I was a slave to his opinion. I drank it.

I don't remember much of what happened after, other than suddenly things began to hurt and ten seconds later whatever it was we were doing was over! I did not know I had lost my virginity until my boyfriend told me what happened. Like most girls, I thought it would be like the movies or television, and I would at least be aware of it when it happened.

I never got to make this decision because I never knew there was a decision to be made. For all intents and purposes, it was a rape with which I completely cooperated. My point here is not what he did, but what it never occurred to me to do. I must emphasize I literally was incapable and unwilling to take care of myself in this situation. It was not his job to read my mind. I am casting no blame here. I simply refused to be my own advocate.

All of those talks I had with my mother were forgotten in the moment, and my only priority was doing what my boyfriend wanted. He was the authority figure in my life, not my mother. There would be consequences if I displeased him: he would leave. There would, of course, be consequences if I displeased my parents, but they would never leave me. They would still love me. Bill might not still love me.

I was a prisoner and a slave to my own perceptions and beliefs. I thought I had no role in my own life. I left everything up to God, and then was confused and scared when God didn't protect me. I had no idea what my role was and what God's role was, and was under the delusion I had no right to assert my own way, and had no choices.

Afterward, he was excited and ecstatic; I was mortified and filled with sorrow. I went home and mourned the loss of my hymen like I had just become an orphan. It meant nothing to me until it was gone.

Now my mother's words rang in my head. I didn't even have the exhilaration of deciding to misbehave for once because I never made that decision. This was the exact point where shame replaced faith and confidence in God and myself. There was nothing in my doctrine to free or encourage anyone. This was my worldview, and I sought out any and all things to reinforce it. I cobbled together a group of Bible verses and sermons I had heard in an effort to earn my way back into Heaven, which dictated my behavior for decades to come.

What I find remarkable and sad is that those who allegedly knew better repeatedly reinforced this bizarre belief. This made me feel even more shame. Even more alone. I wasn't measuring up.

I was just a kid. I needed a guide to set me straight.

I stayed in relationship with this man for ten years. To forgive is divine and being a self-made martyr is even better. Even at that young age, I knew I wasn't all there. We were compatible, I loved him, and I felt guilty for not being more forceful and vocal in my wants, needs, and boundaries. I had no idea what it was to be an advocate for myself. I thought God did it all and I was helpless. My job was just to passively accept whatever came my way.

Fear crept into my life, and peace and purpose slowly ebbed out. My decisions were now based on fear, and most of them were based on fear of losing this person. In my mind, this person had become larger than life, larger than God. He had the power to make me happy or miserable.

I secretly blamed him for all of the things that went wrong, all the paths I didn't take. Of course, in choosing nothing better, I had, in fact, made the choice that would determine the nature of our relationship and every relationship after.

In choosing to do nothing or say nothing to rock the boat, I doomed this relationship. I chose to not be a partner.

In my mind, because adultery was a sin, I had made a lifetime commitment to this person at the age of sixteen. Rather than go to Hell for committing adultery, which I interpreted as having sex, I became the long-suffering wife, without the ring, without the house, and without the perks. With this, I gave Boyfriend the upper hand, and he soon figured out I would do anything and put up with anything rather than end the relationship.

Love became synonymous with fear and meeting someone else's needs and getting their approval. It had nothing whatsoever to do with my own happiness. It had nothing to do with choice.

Without any input from anyone, I decided I would go to Vanderbilt. I took care of the process and told no one until I got in. I fled.

This was also the last "selfish" decision I ever made. I started out really digging into campus life. I made new friends and planned to pledge a sorority. I discovered many of my high school friends were at Vanderbilt, giving me a support system to break out of the relationship.

I met an adorable boy from New Jersey who liked me and could keep up with me. It was fun going on dates that were just dates. Things went well until I talked to Bill on the phone and it was clear I was living my life quite happily. The lies and the threats started, and I never fought back or stood up for myself, in this relationship or any other. In my super-Christian mind, this was the only way. Women were submissive to the men they loved.

Suddenly Bill decided we should be "true to each other," and he threatened me with a break-up if I dated anyone else or pledged a sorority.

I caved. I broke up with my cute Vanderbilt friend. Kappa Delta asked me to pledge, and I really wanted to join. They were wonderful girls and they were allowed to remain who they were. This would have been a great way out of the relationship and on to better friends and experiences. I either couldn't see this as a way out or I refused to see it. In short, I sabotaged my college experience to keep my boyfriend. I was too afraid to risk the screaming, threats, and the breakup.

My boyfriend became my boss and my Higher Power. I had no idea who God was or what he looked like; it might as well be Bill. I thought this was being a good Christian.

Of course, in this environment, my self-esteem plummeted as my fears rose. My internal compass, if I ever had one, was jammed in one direction. I learned I was in this life on my own, alone, unless I was willing to toe the line. No one was going to love or help me if I was not worthy somehow, and it was they who decided I was worthy, not me.

Now, with the wisdom and distance of age, I can see my

life would've been different if I'd had the audacity to "be rude" and call him on this or to challenge the notion that submission was my only option. This pattern of threatening and caving in continued and became what I did with people I loved.

I became a living sacrifice and took comfort in the fact I was burying myself in good works. I transferred to the University of Texas to be nearer to him. In the back of my mind, I knew Vanderbilt had a much better Pre-Med program than the school he was attending, and his parents would be delighted for him to attend, since it was their alma mater. I never mentioned these thoughts to him. He promised he would transfer to UT to be with me instead.

He didn't. Time to bail? Nope. I was "married" in the eyes of God.

In a rare moment of bravery, I confronted him with all the broken promises and said this time I was going to pledge a sorority no matter what he thought. I needed friends. I let the whole idea go after about two months of relentless pressure and threats. Let me stress here, to a large extent, it wasn't he, it was I. I was the victim of mistreatment but I had volunteered for the job! I had cast myself in the role of Joan of Arc, and look how that turned out for her.

My parents had given me a car to navigate the huge UT campus. They had forbidden my using it to go see Bill at his campus, which, of course, I immediately did. Apparently "honor thy father and mother" was not as important as "honor your boyfriend." If I were unavailable on a weekend because I had finals, Bill would threaten to drop me until I went to see him.

Alcohol was present at every single one of our dates because he liked it that way. On one weekend I tried to back out because I had pulled an all-nighter and didn't think I could drive safely with no sleep. His parents happened to be coming to visit that weekend and he was really freaked. He ratcheted up the threats a notch and I went. I fell asleep driving and literally ended up in a ditch. Some Good Samaritans pulled my car out with chains and got me back on the road.

He honestly didn't care. He thought it was funny. At the dinner with his parents, he never mentioned what I had gone through to be with them. At one point during the meal, I fell asleep and toppled out of my chair onto the floor.

Bill responded by humiliating me and reprimanding me. For a brief moment, a fearless me popped out, as I calmly pulled up a chair next to his parents and explained I was operating on two days with no sleep, was in the middle of finals and needed to be studying, and had had a wreck just a couple of hours before on the road to see them.

He never treated me badly in front of his parents again. I had won their respect, even if I didn't have his.

Never once did I take the leap to self-reflection. There was no self to reflect upon. Never once did I look up and ask God if this was what he wanted for me. I assumed this person was in my life because it was divinely ordained, and I had absolutely nothing to say about it! I assumed everything that happened in my life was both divinely ordained and something I had no role or input in at all.

My parents started checking the mileage on the car. This

was a blessing in the form of a Way Out, though I never saw it as anything but an obstacle to bliss. Some of this behavior was just being a teenage girl in love. But a lot of it was a spiritual illness.

Boyfriend's answer to the odometer situation was for me to take the bus at my own expense. I did. It was a ten-hour haul with some of the scariest individuals I have ever seen.

I began realizing this man never came to see me once. It hurt immensely but I believed I was completely powerless to change the situation. I was waiting on God to change things for me, and apparently God didn't want to.

It shames and sickens me to admit this, but my only power over this man was guilt, and when things got really bad I wielded it like a baseball bat. He would feel some remorse but would never give up his position of power. I realize this is where I learned to fear men with power or anyone with power. "Humility" meant to me that I was less than everyone else, and I could expect to be treated accordingly. I could even feel a little righteous and holy for being treated accordingly.

From this point on, if a desirable or even decent man came along and he had anything that would benefit me, I rejected him horribly and cruelly so he could not get power over me and become my God.

My concept of power became extremely warped and, again, I used the Bible as my basis. Everyone in the world, especially men, had all the power, and I had none. I was all alone and no one could help me because I wouldn't let anyone. I wouldn't let them because they might use it against me.

UNDAMNED

I was in Old Testament land and I had put myself there. Unlike the Israelites, there was no escape, no liberator. Everywhere I went, I got my ideas confirmed. Of course, I only went where my ideas would be confirmed. I was punishing myself for breaking the Ten Commandments.

Another perfect escape presented itself. I had applied to law school and, at the last minute, was accepted in August. If I decided to go, I would have to move to San Antonio and be ready to attend classes at St. Mary's in two weeks. I went for it. I went to law school. Of course, we continued to date, so I could poison that environment as well and could have something to feel guilty about.

In law school, I was surrounded by smart, driven young men. I couldn't relate to them in any way that wasn't friendship or extremely casual. By this point love equaled duty, fear, and subservience.

Enter Fred. He was the first person I met in law school. We had a ton in common and became great friends until it became obvious we were developing feelings.

My "Christian" mind warp had taught me love was something I gave but had no right to receive. It was devoid of grace, compassion, or forgiveness. I proceeded to torture this individual for three years *because* I loved him, and in my mind that was a disaster that scared me to death.

This person never did anything bad to me other than love me. But I was locked in a destructive dance of threats, punishment, and Hell. In my mind, I was married to Bill. There was no alternative without punishment, judgment, guilt, and maybe even Hell. I was 21 years old. There was no place in my life for context or perspective, forgiveness or compassion. I was damned and because I was damned, so was everyone who came across my path.

I never explained. I simply avoided Fred and pretended I wasn't interested and suffered and suffered. Every weekend I would leave the one I wanted behind and go see the one I no longer wanted at all. People in law school don't have time for boyfriends, especially long-distance ones. But I made time for one. Love was duty.

It got worse. One night with Bill, we forgot the birth control. He wanted to go ahead, so I did. You guessed it. I found another excuse to deny and punish myself: I became pregnant.

Like an animal that chews off its own leg to get free, I did what I had to do to get free of him. I'm certainly not proud of it. I have tortured myself over this decision for decades upon decades. Others were much more willing to extend grace to me over this fact than I was willing to give to myself. For me, it was just another reason to not trust my "decisions" or myself.

The truth was I had not actually made thoughtful decisions for years. I had let life, my interpretation of a set of Old Testament rules, and threats and simplistic sound bites from other people make my decisions for me.

I worried. I panicked. I reacted. What I didn't do was think, reason it out, or pray. Faith and trust were things I could no longer comprehend. I was a spiritual slave.

After I healed physically from this trauma, I buried it in my mind. The experience went as dormant as my true self. I told no one about this experience. I went to no one for help or guidance.

Enter Shame of Shakespearian proportions…

Previously, I had made my decisions based on fear and duty. Now it was official. I hated myself and behaved accordingly. Now shame joined fear and duty and became my holy Trinity. These were my "go to" reactions and dominated every decision I made. Who needed God? I was doing a tremendous job of judging and punishing myself.

I finally separated from Boyfriend, but that did not fix the problem. There was no me. I was an actress in search of another part to play. My self was bad, so I ran from her as fast and as far as I could.

I fell into cycles of depression, self-hatred, and fear, none of which I let myself feel or acknowledge but all of which ran riot and influenced everything I did. Work and partying became my source of identity. I had to be the best at work, which I wasn't, and then be the best at drinking myself under the table, which I was.

The horrible thing about it, looking back, was my misinterpretation of favorite Bible scriptures, and others' similar misinterpretations, led me to a life without love or dignity. It did not have to be that way. *The pain might have been inevitable, but all of this suffering was completely optional.*

I Now Pronounce You…

CHAPTER 3 🌑 *My Story: Part One*

It was the '80s. Need I say more? *Cosmo* became my new Bible. I behaved like a sailor on leave. I dated every loser in San Antonio and then moved to Austin. I was in the process of dating every loser in Austin when I mercifully met my husband. Mercifully, for me.

The poor man. He had no idea what he was in for. He had no idea the person he was dating wasn't even a person. I had been a slave to other people my whole life. The trajectory of my life could be altered by a disapproving glance from anyone. I assumed everyone on the planet knew more about life, more about faith and more about me, than ME.

Imagine being married to this mindset! My poor husband interfered with my quest for perfection in the Doormat Olympics, and I hated him for it.

It was not until almost middle age that I began to make my escape from this self-imposed slavery and became Undamned and I did it, fighting the one-size-fits-all church every step of the way, and that was a huge part of what God was teaching me.

My life had to be a tragedy for me to be a martyr, and I couldn't get to Heaven unless I was a martyr. I had to get to Heaven, so I could finally have some joy and be who God wanted me to be.

Something was going to have to give if I was going to survive. I had a choice and I finally saw it. I could stay terminally depressed and numb, or I could start to feel all of the ugly feelings I never had let myself feel, and see what happened. That's when the shit really hit the fan.

The Tipping Point/Keys to the Cage

There is nothing like failure to bring about a transformation. I was failing in my marriage. I was failing as a mother. I had already failed in my career. The traumas I had previously ignored and buried were surfacing. On a daily basis I was filled with despair and fear. I couldn't look back on my life without so much regret that I would begin to consider my life hopeless and meaningless. I had been clinically depressed for a decade, and until this point it seemed perfectly reasonable.

It never occurred to me it might have something to do with how I treated myself and how I let others treat me. I found it increasingly difficult to be "meek" or what I thought the Bible meant by "meek." I hated the patsy I saw in the mirror every morning. Queen of the doormats started to get a little bit angry.

O.M.G. I did not know where else to go. I was programmed to go to others for answers and approval. This was my last-ditch effort to get someone else to validate and tell me how to live my life. In I walked to McChurch.

I loved it! I chose a church that was hip and looked unconventional because it looked like who I wanted to be. My discernment in this area turned out to be a tad off.

Slowly, it dawned on me the things God had called on me to do for decades were the very things I had been judged and criticized for doing my whole life. I now knew my fear of losing approval had kept me from doing God's will. I also knew I was weak and would need a spiritual community to have my back while I faced these fears and tried to grow.

I began to see the truth about my life and myself, and that

made me bolder and less fearful, which gave me confidence to speak the truth. Since denial had been my escape, I knew I had to speak the truth often, no matter how ugly, to keep myself grounded in reality.

But McChurch did not agree. It was "unseemly" to wonder the things I wondered aloud.

Deep down in my bones, I felt God wanted my husband and me to temporarily separate in order to save our marriage, not break it up. It was clear we were powerless to do anything to help ourselves. It seemed to me God was driving the bus, and he wanted to be able to get to each of us separately and renew our hearts and minds before we came together again, healed of the things that made our relationship toxic. Nothing else was going to save it.

It was about taking a step in faith and trusting God to do what seemed almost impossible, but stepping and trusting were not things I did unless I could forecast a result. I was a lawyer in my professional life, so planning for the worst-case scenario was second nature. My husband and I were in a stranglehold of hurt and resentment from which we alone could not free ourselves, and it would not stop if we both didn't take our hands off of the situation long enough for God to come in and put his hands on it.

Finally I saw The Lesson for my life God had been placing before my eyes forever, but from which I had always fled: I had always cared more about what mankind thought of me and my actions than what God thought.

Before there could ever be hope of improvement, I had to

admit things were bad. I was so relieved and filled with peace with that divine revelation. I knew what I needed to say and do! I was so happy and peaceful. My miracle was about to happen! I had put my relationship with my husband and my kids ahead of my relationship with God. God sent me a little reality check: "Hey, who gave you this man and these kids in the first place?"

But when I shared this conviction with my spiritual community, my story got turned upside down and backwards. People pointed fingers in my face or shook their heads as they walked away. I got the Ten Commandments and the scriptures about love and adultery with which I had harmed myself for decades.

The question I kept asking was, "How do you know when enough is enough?"

At one point, a friend and church elder bluntly told me I was going to Hell, no matter which choice I made. She put suicide on a par with separation. Not divorce. Separation.

This triggered such outrage that finally I began to question what I was being told. I was not an adulterer! I was not divorced!

What had I done? I had admitted I was having significant marital problems and had been for fifteen years. I admitted I was exhausted from taking on the responsibility for the success of my marriage and what people thought of it and me by extension, and I was going to give it to God. I knew this was not a sin.

Even though I started to question things, I was new to

defending my choices and still addicted to approval. I did not know simply walking away was an acceptable option.

I stayed and fought. At first I got arguments, then I got nothing. Radio Silence. To love myself, accept myself, and defend myself from unacceptable behavior and projected shame from others, God wanted me to see that incurring disapproval and occasionally being "rude" was not only necessary, but also exactly what he wanted. I wanted my marriage to be joyful and good more than anything.

That's when I got another Lesson: I was trying to affect something that was in God's hands. I had placed myself in the role of God. I had placed others' perceptions in the role of God.

I never got an answer from anyone in authority in McChurch. It was like I was speaking to the automated Jack in the Box® at the fast-food restaurant of the same name.

Is it any wonder I finally blew my top at McChurch?
I was struggling to finally be born. To be born as the person God knew I was, but I didn't. I needed someone to walk with me and be brave, because I knew people would disapprove, but I also knew this is what God wanted me to do, to risk disapproval for once, for him.

Something Had to Give, and Boy, Did It!
The original author of the ironic twist provided a path no human could ever dream up. Redemption came in the form of someone whose jerk-like behavior infuriated me beyond all reason. That forced me to rely on my own understanding of God and what he was doing in my life: finally.

I went to talk to my pastor at the time about the fact my life was unlivable and I was following the Bible and its teachings. I believed my marriage was at the point where things were going to change for the better or worse and I was supposed to do something to change it, but I wasn't sure what to do. I wanted permission to step away from my marriage and let God have it. I sought confirmation God could work in this way. At the very least I wanted guidance and a sounding board.

I did what I always did: deferring to others, refusing to be an advocate for myself, and being submissive to men in authority.

The pastor refused to talk to me about the most important and pivotal issue in my life. In a weary tone of voice he said, "Do you even understand it isn't about you?" and handed me off to someone else. I have no way of knowing what he intended or what he was thinking, and I choose to believe this was uttered with the intent of revealing a beneficial lesson.

To be fair, I was being somewhat of an ass, expecting answers in a few minutes between services. What I felt at first was shame–for a millisecond. I felt the heat of embarrassment rise to my face and then... I was mad as hell.

This turned out to be the best thing that could have happened to me. I am so grateful to this person for treating me in this way; it resulted in a completely new outlook for me.

I felt like Dorothy in *The Wizard of Oz* when she finally sees what is behind the curtain. I decided to quit taking everything offered at face value as Divine Truth and take the most important relationship of my life–that of me with my

Maker–into my own hands. I stopped giving others the right to be "talking heads" in my life and destiny.

I owe my whole new outlook to this person and his undoubtedly unintentional remark. He was a nice person having a really bad day, colliding with me having a bad day. God used him and his actions to communicate to me what no one else could: My opinion about what is going on in my life and how God shows himself in my circumstances has as much value as anyone else's. This encounter also provoked me to wonder exactly how many times I had treated others in the same way: seeing them and their stories in some kind of abbreviated version, so I could hurry up and give the advice or come to the conclusion I thought the situation and the person warranted.

This was where I really got the fact I was in a cage, and my spiritual destiny was not for others to decide.

The problem was not the doctrine of that church. The problem was I tried to fit my life into the tiny confines of its doctrine. I had outgrown it.

It was like a spiritual and artistic volcano, long dormant, suddenly is awakened. I was undammed and undamned, and heaven help anyone blocking the spiritual flow. Spiritual poetry spewed out of me like a malfunctioning fountain. I couldn't stop it. I could see life with the eyes of a child again. Lots of the poems were angry and resembled Eminem more than Jesus, but they were a necessary way of calling the bullshit for what it was.

The approval junky who became a lawyer because it sounded good became a somewhat disreputable artist–a laughingstock by my own old definition–and it freed me. Daily I practiced unmasking, confronting, and telling the truth. It was easier to do in poetry, because there was an art form between the recipient of my truth and me.

That daily practice introduced me to God in a way that going to church and merely reading the Scriptures never did. It taught me to feel and actually experience the Bible by putting it in my own words, in my own context. My writings became a living testament of God's daily impact in my life. I was never going to turn my soul or my salvation over to another human being again.

I separated very briefly from my husband.

Everyone, including me, began to grow up and take responsibility for themselves.

But my church told me I was sinning and selfish. The reaction was as if I had come in and told them I thought having multiple husbands would save my marriage. Now, of course, I see the pain of this rejection was necessary to finish my hunger for others' approval once and for all.

What they saw was a pain in the ass, and I was. That was their context: quick evaluation and judgment. I was grieving the loss of my pretend self, my pretend husband, and my pretend marriage, and while facing fear and the unknown, I was brutally honest about it. I had also come to grips with the truth about a lot of things I had willfully refused to see, and that was painful. That was *my* context. I was lamenting as they do in the Bible, so I could heal.

Context was everything in this situation.

It was sacred.

That was the lesson.

I had left my brain and my dignity in the collection plate, and it was time to retrieve it. I resolved to save and undamn myself.

Scriptural Excavation, Demolition, and Repair

I resolved to find evidence in the Scriptures and in my own life that I was, in fact, a loving and loveable human being.

At glacial speed I realized being a lawyer involved at least a few gifts. I could analyze. I could think for myself. I could defend others and had been my whole life. Why not defend or at least make a case for myself?

On a fact-finding mission, I studied the Bible harder than any law book. I studied it like my life depended on it.

What I found was a whole other Bible. I found evidence of a whole other God up there, too. One who was in my corner and did not hate me or want me to be a slave of anyone.

I found a mountain of evidence that God wanted to emancipate me. He wanted me to be Undamned. He wanted me to see the other side of the coin. I wasn't a mistake. I could stop doing penance. It became clear that God didn't want it.

I literally had to lose and turn my back on my religion to find God. It had been blocking my view of him.

The God I found was the God of the 139th Psalm.

>*God, I am an open book to you;*
>*even from a distance you know what I am thinking...*

UNDAMNED

> *At night, I'm immersed in the light!*
> *It's a fact: darkness isn't dark to you…*
> *You shaped me first inside,*
> *Then out…*
> *Body and soul, I am marvelously made…*
> *You know me inside and out,*
> *You know every bone in my body:*
> *You know exactly how I was made…*
> *How I was sculpted from nothing into something.*
> *Please, God, do away with all the men and women who belittle you, Infatuated with cheap god-imitations…*[21]

My God is bigger than "the rules." To say otherwise is to belittle and limit him. He is most certainly bigger than McChurch and its doctrine.

I had been worshipping somebody else's God. I had been getting down on my knees and worshipping the book itself, instead of trying to understand how it applied to me individually. I had made the Bible a list of rules I must follow to get to Heaven. I had missed the overall message. A list of rules eliminated any need for discretion, risk, or discernment in my life.

I began the process of God- and self-discovery. I found two scriptures that saved me. They saved me by indicating, perhaps, God was not about The Rules, or praying publicly on Twitter or Facebook, or generic, generalized anything.

1) Isaiah 55:8, NIV

> *"For my thoughts are not your thoughts, and my ways*

are not your ways," declares the Lord…

God doesn't just say it, he declares it. He makes a special point about context, his context.

Who am I to second-guess what God tells, teaches, and shows me?

Who am I to reduce him to someone else's experience and understanding?

Who am I to listen to "talking heads," or even learned teachers, and not listen to God?

Who am I to hire an interpreter for what he is saying plainly, again and again?

2) Isaiah 54:10, NIV

"Though the mountains be shaken and the hills be removed, yet my unfailing love for you will not be shaken nor my covenant of peace be removed," says the Lord, who has compassion on you.

God has compassion on me. God loves me. God has my back. I can trust in what he is teaching and showing me.

I can trust my own individual experience, **because** it is individual and unique, not in spite of it.

Seeing a chink in McChurch's armor was a wonderful opportunity to be responsible for my own soul and salvation. This happened because God cared about my life like no church could. Moreover, he was in my life, making his presence known in all of the chaos, making his wishes known.

It turned out to be simple, in a whole different way. It was all about the angle and about healing and reconciliation to God. For me, the story of the Bible was about the oppressed and the exiled finally coming home to be reconciled with their God. He wasn't punishing me. He was waiting for me. He had been waiting for me my whole life.

I discovered a God of freedom and flexibility and flow who was bigger than I had let him be. This God viewed me as his sacred creation today, as I was, and it was not conditional on making an audition or fitting some demographic criteria.

I had been looking for a parable to show me the way and tell me what to do, but I was the parable! I was the woman at the well, looking for redemption, acceptance, and transformation. I was looking to change my life and make it worth living and, perhaps, even worth emulating. I was looking for Jesus with skin on, but what I actually found was Jesus and myself.

It was about daring to be unique in an environment of conformity.

It was about finding the place where I belonged, not where I somehow managed to fit in.

God didn't want me to do the expedient or polite thing. He didn't want me to make my friends feel good at my own expense. He didn't want me to hide my pain and grief so no one would feel uncomfortable.

He wanted me to be more like Jesus. He wanted me to refuse to conform, and not accept crumbs. He wanted me to grow up, yes, but he wanted me to go through all of the stages of growth. I went through my terrible twos and spiritual adolescence before I could be fully formed spiritually. It wasn't pleasant for anyone, but it was necessary.

God arranged to have me experience rejection, confrontation, punishment, exile of sorts, and being left alone to help free me from the fear of those things, and to see there is something worse: losing myself and my personal relationship with God.

My greatest flaw also was my greatest gift: My mouth was my salvation. I had to hear the truth out of my own mouth before I could recognize the truth and know it for what it was. I was still a long way from living my own personal truth. I still didn't want to get in trouble! I valued staying out of the line of fire more than I valued myself. But once I started speaking truth I couldn't stop.

Now, looking back at the experiences of my life, I can see what I was told about that provision in 1st Corinthians about love, and what I told myself, was someone else's lesson. Not mine. My lesson was the direct opposite. God wanted me to have love, not just give it. God wanted me to love myself as he loved me.

Now I see those provisions, which were a death sentence for so many years, as something freeing. It's not about duty, earning grace, being a martyr.

It's not about what I do at all.

It's about whom I love.

Do I love God? Check.

Do I love others and aim to see them as God sees them? Check.

Do I love myself and see myself as God sees me? Finally,

check.

Now, I see this provision is about acceptance and grace. The very things I was looking for. Finally, I get it.

So, what I'm sure looked like a mid-life rebellion to my church was actually God's perfect timing, as one layer at a time of my self-delusion and woundedness was exposed, lovingly removed, and healed.

Why on earth would I have entrusted my spiritual path to anyone other than my Source and expected good results?

The Angle

In a way, I do owe part of my salvation to McChurch. My experiences there reopened all of my old wounds–the ones I had simply slapped a Band-Aid on and ignored–and instead of covering them over again and submitting, my anger kept them open and let the infection get out. These wounds eventually healed, because they were cleaned out and exposed to the open air. These experiences taught me I could and should separate myself from others' opinions and feelings. God taught me to rely on him instead of other humans with feet of clay.

I chose to embrace being human and cooperate in my own spiritual development and maturation by following these steps:

Self-love and acceptance
Humility
Surrender to my higher power
Receiving forgiveness/grace/love/acceptance
Gratitude
Transforming myself at every opportunity

Loving my fellow humans and God
Freedom and confidence in self and God
Assisting in the transformation of others

Taking each step in order allowed me to eventually grow up. As I went through adolescence, I got angry when my own boundaries were hurled in my face, when I asked for help and guidance and got "correction." I was outraged and revolted when told I had sinned when I hadn't. It took something this extreme to finally see myself as an equal to everyone else, and to give myself a vote in my own life.

Just as a teenage girl begins to question rules that seem too restrictive or imply a lack of trust, I began to question things. Loudly.

If I believed I was called by God to do a specific thing, and asked for and received confirmation that I believed to be from God of this calling, how could that be wrong?

Why would someone who didn't know me from a hole in the ground tell me I was wrong?

How dare they say that?

What do they know?

Why is 'leadership' the answer to whatever question I ask?

Not attractive. But necessary.

...And you know what? It wasn't the condemnation, advice, preaching, or discipline that undamned and saved me– it was the *anger, righteous anger.* For some, anger leads down the path of destruction, but that is their context.

In the context of my life, righteous anger has turned out to be somewhat sacred. It has the power to move me out of paralysis. It makes me aware God values and loves me and does not consider me a punching bag for others.

Righteous anger moved me past the fear and paralysis into action. It was the key to healing, redemption, forgiveness, and it gave me grace and hope for a better future. The cynical pit-bull to whom life was all about power or the lack thereof stopped caring about power and started pursuing joy.

I started a poetry website to which I think maybe twenty people subscribed. I started going to open-mic nights, and spoken word and poetry competitions. I was still a little afraid, but I did not let the fear stop me. I was afraid of sucking, but I was no longer afraid of punishment for just being me. I was developing a backbone.

This was exactly the person I was before I committed spiritual suicide.

I had begun writing poetry and songs when I was ten years old. I had forgotten all of these years that it was my first love, my way of processing the events in my life, and my way of talking to and hearing from God.

When I looked in the mirror, I got a reality check. Others treated the Bible like it was God, instead of a dynamic living document, relevant in every situation. *But I had treated it that way, too!*

Others worshipped the symbols of faith, instead of the author of faith. *But so was I. I had reduced God to three scriptures.*

Duh. It was time for me to wake up and see God wasn't just in church. I didn't necessarily have to visit him there.

He was in and all around me. He wasn't just in the Bible. He was with me and for me every day, here in the present. I had been valiantly attempting to freeze-dry and shrink God to fit inside my Bible, especially the Old Testament part and its list of things to do to be "perfect."

The context of my life made it different from any of the leaders I approached for wisdom. There was no malice. It wasn't their fault, but mine. I had expected divine behavior and insight from people. It was simply beyond their personal life experience. Without realizing it, I had set them up to fail by making them idols.

Because I revered all religious leaders as mystical saints, I did not go through the process of discerning who was trustworthy and who wasn't. I couldn't see they were just being human, something I would not allow them to be. God is everything or God is nothing. Once I believed and trusted this, I saw a way out.

Actually, all I had to do was turn the corner, and everything I imagined and prayed for was there. But to turn the corner, I had to cross the threshold to see there was a corner. Truth telling requires practice once you've been trained away from doing it. (Children do it naturally.)

I learned "rest" is an active verb. Once I rested in the Truth, Love, Power, and Protection that was God, I began to receive the hunger for him for which I had prayed for so long. It was enough to be in his presence. I had always thought that sounded stupid, but it was true. I began to receive a small measure of the wisdom and discernment I had prayed for and as a result, saw the scriptures as they truly were. I didn't need an interpreter. I saw them as life giving and hopeful, not as the walls to a cage.

When I sought him just for him, I began to find and see all the things I had missed before. He and Truth were all around me and within me. All I had to do was rest in him, and the answers gradually came. He knew living rigorously in the Truth was a life skill I would have to re-develop. I had to practice seeking, recognizing, speaking, and living in the Truth gradually.

Because God not only loved me, but also was Love, I found the self-compassion and forgiveness I sought. I found the self-love I had thrown away because I thought it was wrong.

I realized I was simply doing the best I could with the tools I had at the time. When I quit looking to self-help gurus and "experts" to fix me, I saw I already had all the necessary tools within me and at my disposal.

Strange as it may sound, my chronic shyness began to dissipate as I viewed my fellow humans less as Goliaths to my David, locked in mortal combat. My relationships became more peaceful as I became more peaceful. The Kingdom really was within me.

I didn't have to worry about my personal power vis-a-vis anyone else, once I realized I never had it to begin with. I had no influence or control over other people. Trying to stoically muscle through my interactions and problems was futile and had messed up my life. What a waste, when all I had to do was look up and ask for strength and protection to access the source of infinite power and strength that has my back.

Less is more.

In quietness and trust is your strength, but you would have none of it.[22]

I had to learn wisdom and discernment on my own to see that God wasn't damning me. He was offering me freedom from the rules and my addiction to them.

I lost my church and got a true sanctuary.

Now, I'm still small before my Creator, but I'm not powerless, helpless, or insignificant among his creations.

God envisioned and planned a bigger life for me than I thought I deserved. God waited for me to grow up and stand up on my own two feet. He let me go through each stage of the spiritual life cycle in sequence, so I would be able to handle the pain, the healing, and the growth. He let me stay in adolescence long enough to grow a pair. He repeatedly encouraged me to observe that the perfectly behaved didn't always behave and were never perfect. He wanted me to quit listening to "learned" advice long enough to hear him. He allowed me to stop making appointments and pilgrimages to see him once a week, long enough to feel his presence on a daily basis. His wish for me was to finally cease worshipping religion and its trappings and worship him. He dared me to risk the things I feared for him, to find freedom. He gave me the strength and trust to risk losing my security to find my true strength in him.

That which is to give light must endure burning.
~Victor Frankl

There was something else he urged me to do: Face my fears

and write this book. My journey to the truth was so painful. Denial, poll taking, and approval seeking were easy for me. Truth had to be more than words for me. I had to live it. If I wrote it all down and released it into the world, I could not retreat or run from it.

In summary, the pastor was right. My life wasn't about my circumstances, my heroes, or me. It wasn't about my husband or my marriage, either. It wasn't about the one-size-fits-all church. It was about transformation. It was about becoming a spiritual adult, about discovering, claiming, and defending my personal story and using it for the greater good as a parable of transformation, redemption, and hope.

I believe each of us is a parable Jesus uses to teach, and transform – not just us, but others. The very thing that makes us of use to God and others is our personal struggle and experience. That is our ministry. That is our calling. Our Yes or No either damns or saves us.

As I grew up spiritually, I realized the walls I'd created so long ago were actually projections of how I felt about myself. I reinforced these projections with scriptures, religious teachings, and opinions of others that I did not filter or examine to determine their truth.

Once these new truths finally sank in, I saw I was the architect of my cage. I created the blueprints and could have escaped at any time.

Once it became clear I was the architect, I walked out of that cage, I burned it down, I burned the blueprints, and I haven't looked back.

I had faced McChurch; now it was time to finally face myself, and make sure I remained free.

CHAPTER FOUR

Extreme Spiritual Makeover
Part Two: The Big Reveal

It takes one a long time to become young
~ Pablo Picasso

The Japanese have a gorgeous word, *kintsukuroi*, referring to mending broken pots with gold. The word means "golden repair," and implies something is more beautiful for having been broken. That's how I now feel about others and myself. I now understand God never wastes a hurt.

I remind myself of this frequently. It's like being born: weird, scary, and uncomfortable, but there is no alternative if one is going to be a member of the human race. The painful, anxiety- provoking crises I have faced were preludes to being born and growing into a new phase of my life. Writing out the narrative of the high and low points of my life gave me insight and self-compassion, but I noticed something even more helpful: Only one person controls the narrative of my life: I do. That means no matter what happens, good or bad, I am the biggest obstacle I face.

The narrative of my life had been devoid of the word or even the concept of "today." Now "today" is all I allow myself to consider. Today is the only thing I have any power over at all. It is all God gives me. The rest belongs to him. But today is a lot. I can do and endure things for 24 hours that would be impossible if I forecast them into the future. By focusing on today, I am allowing God the opportunity to change my tomorrow by getting out of the way.

In talking to a lot of people who couldn't listen, understand, or help, I found a core group of people whom I consider my sanctuary and my "checks and balances." Healing allowed me to turn my back on the past and to focus on staying in the present. I cultivate and guard this safe group of people because it is essential to my staying out of lies and denial. If I'm going through something I can't bear to tell anyone, I confide in one of these trusted friends so I can prevent the situation from festering into a secret and a sickness.

In writing my life, I finally saw the trajectory of my life. Newly emancipated, undammed, and undamned, I was determined to adopt a lifestyle that would keep me free from this religious addiction. This chapter describes how I learned a whole new life.

Because I knew of no specific recovery program in existence for my particular addiction, I adopted a new lifestyle of freedom.

I made a conscious decision to do everything differently.

I asked God what I should do and how I should do it. He revealed all of the delusions and lies in my life, the times that I had betrayed myself. The first step was to own up to all of the lies, replacing them with the truth proclaimed from my own mouth as often as necessary. No more hiding in denial and untruths to avoid acting or deciding.

The first lie was that I suffered from something that had an intellectual cure. Not. I was a religious addict and I needed to find a spiritual cure. I threw out my self-help books and looked for God-given tools to help me. I resolved to no longer ignore the tools already in my possession, simply because they were unique to me or because they were not heralded by a choir of angels. Maybe I was making it more difficult than it needed to be.

I designed a spiritual detox program that would renew my mind, deprogram my shaming and limiting beliefs, and give me freedom and joy by excavating my true inner child from this false self I had been constructing all of these years. It was a collage of wisdom I had heard, seen and experienced from literally every place and situation in which I found myself. I was ready to learn and there were lessons everywhere. These are the steps I followed. I didn't follow them one at a time, but all at once. Working them in sequence didn't work. I needed a comprehensive, holistic approach: a totally new lifestyle.

The second lie was that I was both humble and altruistic. I now aim to cultivate an attitude of true humility for completely selfish reasons: because my happiness level is in direct proportion to my humility.

I'm not talking about what I mistakenly believed was humility; i.e., thinking everyone else is better. Submission had been a highly charged term in my life, and I confused humility with submissiveness. But I have discovered it is necessary for me to submit my ideas, my perceptions, and my will to God and only God.

This kind of submission makes things work. It leaves me with an open mind and clearer perceptions of what is going on in my life. If I am submitted to God and only God, then I will not fall prey to hero worship, idolatry, or being misled or deceived.

Humility gives me the capability to receive from God both blessings and lessons. If I am humble, as I define it, I am open and available to be taught. I am open to the idea that I don't know. It's difficult, but if I do this, I don't have to search for happiness or peace. They find me on their own. They fall on and around me like rain. I have unclenched my fists so I can receive whatever God wants me to, and I am capable, at least at times, of letting happiness happen.

Before, I searched for happiness but never found it because it was pre-defined in my mind. So many times I had missed it because it didn't look like what I thought it should.

Directly related to humility is my traditional practice of trying to fix myself, fix things, fix people, and figure things out. It took a long time for me to see that this is arrogance. I can't even be sure I know what my own character defects are from day to day. How can I single-handedly fix them in others? Hands off! Others are not my domain. They have a God, too, and he takes care of them.

The only way my character is going to ever change is through sustained contact with God, where I ask him to help me change my defects, and he does. He gets to decide what needs fixing and how to fix it, and I get to put his plan in action. This gives me clarity on what I need from God at any given moment and keeps me from replacing it with what I want. It is his.

The same goes for figuring things out, when I assume I know best and I know everything there is to know about a situation. How often is that actually true? Never.

Related to this arrogance is my motivation. Am I helping someone by "fixing" him or her? Do they really need fixing, or do I want to make myself more comfortable with choices and behavior that are theirs alone to own?

If I start feeling overwhelmed and anxious for someone else, I ask myself: *What am I trying to do? Is it mine to do?* (It never is!) The more telling question is: *What do I want to get by making them change?*

Half the time, what I am striving for is none of my business. Being a person of faith doesn't mean I get to dictate anyone else's. When I am feeling fearful for or about a loved one, I now make it work for me, forever the actor in search of a role, by asking, *What is my motivation?*

The third lie I decided to face and replace was my perception that I was strong, and knew what my strengths were. This was a tall order. My armor made me appear strong and invulnerable, like I knew what was going on, but it kept me from feeling, healing, or giving/receiving love. My true strengths are the vulnerability and honesty of the child living in me. This requires trusting God and myself.

Task One: Face Vengeful God, Fire Him, and Replace Him With a God of My Understanding

Whom would I replace him with? I had no idea how to go about trusting God, but I knew what I needed from God in order to trust him. I needed him to be less of a ruler or even a father figure and more like a best friend. I needed him to be an advocate for me like I never really was for myself. I saw glimmers of this kind of God in my scriptural research conducted in the last chapter.

I resolved to start thinking of him this way and institute some practices to bolster and enhance this idea. I decided to treat myself as a loving Higher Power would, with gentleness, acceptance, and compassion. He would love me unconditionally. He would forgive, not punish.

I started in the smallest possible way. I didn't know who God was or who I was, but I did know the antidote to the pervasive shame I had felt in the past was a new feeling of worthiness, and the belief I deserved God's attention. I began engaging in the following practice:

Every morning when I woke up and was still in that place that felt close to God, I would march into my bathroom, look at myself in the mirror, and audibly tell myself:

> *God loves you right now, just the way you are, and so do I. I forgive you.*
> *I will never let you down again.*
> *I will be here for you, no matter what.*
> *I will listen to you.*
> *I hear you when you cry and I see you when you hurt, and I will hold you until the hurt*
> *goes away.*
> *I will fight for you.*
> *I will put you first, because you are worthy of my time.*
> *You are God's child and his priority.*
> *He is waiting to hear from you.*

This simple practice was so powerful that for months I could rarely meet my own eyes. On the few occasions I could, they were full of tears. I felt that child's pain and saw her mourning the loss of her faith, the loss of her God, her childhood, and herself. Over time, it became easier and easier to treat her with acceptance and tenderness. I embraced her and comforted her the way God embraces and comforts me.

The only way I could feel loved and accepted by my Higher Power was to show myself the love, compassion, acceptance, and gentleness my Higher Power longs to shower upon me. I resigned as God's distributor of judgment, wisdom, and blessings, especially to myself, because I had been doing a crappy job.

Despite the fact I had always thought focusing on myself was selfish and evil, doing just that was the key to liberation, redemption, and celebration. Focusing on others, their needs, their judgments, and their words, while ignoring my own once felt humble and right to me, but it no longer did.

I lost a lot of fear and gained some discernment. I wasn't the greatest sinner there ever was. I wasn't even the biggest mess. I wanted to be unique but I wasn't. Once I realized how much like everyone else I really was, I could look my reflection in the eye and love her. Once I started loving that brave but misguided child in the mirror, I could believe my Higher Power loved her, too. I grew larger and became right-sized compared to my fellow man. Others' words and judgments ceased to sting so much.

The negative What Ifs were replaced with:

> *What if God just wants me to be happy?*
> *What if I am enough?*
> *What if I knew everything is going to work together for my good?*

> *What could happen if I am truly willing?*
> *What if God approves of me, even if I'm not perfect?*
> *What if my inability to imagine and embrace what God has in store for me is the only thing limiting my life?*
> *What if I'm going to find whatever I look for, good or bad?*

I began to live my life accordingly and kept questioning everything I had once believed to be true.

I had always believed in God, Jesus, the holy catholic church, the Ten Commandments, the whole shebang. It had always been a source of comfort and the basis of both superiority and inferiority. It was such a great story.

It never occurred to me that *how* I believed was at least as important as what I believed and recited by rote. It never occurred to me my love of stories and storytelling had caused me to tell myself an untrue story about God.

I had supplied God's features based on my experience and imagination, my Bible, things my parents told me, and hellfire and brimstone. In part, I also based him on myself and on my fears of humiliation, judgment, and punishment. There was no room in my story for the idea that redemption had already happened in the here and now. But that was the truth. What I had been searching for had already arrived on the day I was born.

I asked God to show me the Truth. This meant mastering the art of surrender, a heretofore-alien concept for me. I could only accomplish the former by writing it down here. Doing so helped me see the untruths I had been telling myself, heal from the hurts, perceive my part in them, and actually see evidence that someone up there had been watching out for me. I dived into the tried-and-true 12 Steps that have proved to be the bedrock of recovery for so many addicts, particularly the first three.

Step 1 was admitting my life was unmanageable and I was powerless. Step Two was believing a higher power could *restore* me to sanity. Well, that implied recognition that things needed to return to sanity. It was pretty easy to list the crazy things in my life and the crazy things I did, and to admit it was all too much for me. I had already discovered my belief system and religion were unmanageable and actually harmful, and that my family life was dysfunctional, to say the least.

But my ideas about my limitations and myself were wacky too. I had really believed I could control my loved ones and keep them safe and happy if I lived their lives for them and ignored myself.

My concept of personal integrity was both absolute and impossible. My concept of truth was insane and false. A good portion of the brick and mortar of my cage was my childish concept of integrity and my worship of words, if they were anyone else's but mine.

Working Step 1 and repeatedly asking to be shown the truth in every situation and problem led me to be more flexible and open.

Step 2: I came to believe a Higher Power of my understanding could restore me to sanity.

Step 3: I made a decision to turn my will and my life over to the care of my Higher Power. This was where the rubber met the road. Since so much of my life was my religion and concept of God, I had to give these up too and be willing to let my Higher Power replace them. Steps 2 and 3 were harder and they exposed another lie to face and replace: I hadn't trusted God with anything at all. I didn't trust that old God because I was afraid of him. I had created all this protective armor, this false self who was the sentinel and guardian of everything and everybody, so I wouldn't have to turn anything over to God. This was and is my daily, hourly struggle. Trust.

Treating myself as a loving Higher Power would helped me to gradually take Steps 2 and 3. Something else helped, too: Someone with similar religious experience suggested I substitute the word, "could" in Step 2 with "would."

I could and can believe my new Higher Power, who was also my best friend, would restore me to sanity! Sometimes, though, I can only do it in ten-minute increments. How did I learn to surrender?

By admitting and accepting total defeat. There simply has to be a better way than my way. This is the beginning of unimaginable freedom.

I pray before my feet hit the floor in the morning for my Higher Power's will, the discernment to see it, and the strength to carry it out. I repeat this prayer any time I feel confused or frustrated, which is often.

I constantly and vigilantly keep myself in the present,

minute by minute. I am able to achieve this only by doing three things:

> I use my inner child as the gateway to surrender. As a neurotic adult, I could not do it, but I could as a child. And I am a child, still, of God.
>
> I use prayer as a substitute for worrying, planning, self-shaming, and self-flagellating. I treat prayer as the most active verb I know. I don't pretend I'm not worried, scared, whatever; I tell God I am, give the matter to him, then move on.
>
> I set a stopwatch for an hour at a time. Before I set it, I pray for God's will, then I do what I believe he is leading me to do, with total concentration for one hour. This reminds me I can surrender only the present moment. If I look too far into the future, I'm taking it back from God.

I trusted God with little things first. "God, which way should I take to work?" "God, I'm so tired, could you please help me?" "God, could you help me interact with this person in a way that blesses us both?"

I remember two expressions that keep things in perspective and put a smile on my face: "If you don't let go, you will get dragged" and "If you're trying, you're dying." If I find myself trying "to make things work," they don't work! I let God take over.

I keep in mind the concept of the blind corner. A lot of people use the analogy of steps or a ladder to illustrate how to surrender; i.e., "Just take that first step." For me, the idea of a corner is much more helpful. The fact I may not be able to see where I am going, or see anything as I trust God to lead me, does not mean nothing is there. It means my view is obstructed. All I need to do is to turn the corner for what I was missing to become clear. Everything I have prayed and hoped for may be just on the other side of that corner. But there is only one way to do it: blindly and with faith.

Because I have a tendency to live and die by how much I get accomplished on my "To Do" list, if I don't surrender to God and let him decide what is for me to do and what isn't, I'm sunk. The items on my list can take on the nature of "Thou Shalts" until I completely lose perspective and begin to feel shame for not finishing the list. I will not and cannot afford to let shame back into my life, even over a little thing like a list.

After prayer and surrendering the items I think I have to do today to God, I ask, "Is this something only I can do?" If not, I let it go.

If the answer is yes, I ask, "Does this have to be done today?" If not, there is still plenty of time for God to work it out without my meddling. If it is in the future, then it isn't mine to do today. It might not even be mine to do ever. I can't know. This doesn't mean I abdicate being a responsible adult, stop buying home insurance, or quit my job.

I ask God what the truth is about every situation, person, goal about which I have confusion or intensity, and with every single "negative" emotion, like fear, resentment, anxiety, or confusion. Sometimes, it takes more time than I would like to receive clarity, but it does eventually come.

For me, Steps 1, 2, and 3 are a waltz, with all the steps intertwined and working together. I don't separate them from each other. The answers to how I would be able to surrender and turn over my life came with the consistent conscious practice of contact with God. *It was the answer to everything.* It is the source of all power in my life. There is no direction, no revelation, no truth, no love, and certainly no peace without my being in the presence of a loving God.

Although I had prayed my whole life, I had been praying in a way that prevented me from knowing God or thinking of him as a friend. My prayers had been lists of things to do to keep me happy, keep me from being anxious or fearful, give me courage, give me this, and give me that. I had treated God like a Pez dispenser in the sky. I had spent a long time in prayer, confessing my sins and failings, which only reinforced the idea I was unlovable and unworthy of his time.

I resolved to pray to God in a new way, to not just talk at him, but also be willing to hang out with him as I would a friend. To be willing to sacrifice some stage time and give up my monologue to allow him into the dialogue.

I had no idea how to pray this new way, so I decided to journal by writing to my Higher Power. Every morning, I would pour out to H.P. whatever came to mind, and after a page or two, the static in my mind would empty onto the paper, and I would find myself confessing the innermost desires of my heart and my secret dreams. I could talk to him like a best friend, if I wrote it down. After a couple more pages,

I was emotionally spent, felt great, thanked him, and stopped. I read over what I had written and realized my writings had formed prayers. True prayers. Not Pharisee-like playacting, or self-flagellation and groveling, nor had I barked orders to my Higher Power. I had passionately confessed my true heart and revealed it as if he were my best friend.

A really amazing thing happened after a few weeks of this practice: He started answering. As I drew closer to him, he drew closer to me. As the weeks passed, I noticed my writings contained more questions than declarations. In my very small way, I was beginning to ask his will in certain situations. "I don't know what to do. What should I do?" "I can't do this. Can you help me?"

If I slowed down long enough to simply take a few deep meditative breaths, read over my questions, and wait a few minutes, the answer often came. Frequently, it came in writing. I would read the questions, and my hand would just write the answers. Just as frequently the answers would come when I least expected it during the day, when my guard was down. It is freakish how often these answers came when I was in the shower or sitting in an even more vulnerable position. My best friend wouldn't stand on ceremony or refuse to talk to me because I was in an awkward position.

Every day as I sat with pen in hand, I would write, "God, this is my will," and I would pour it all out onto the page. I would write everything I wanted and needed, and then I would write, "I surrender my will today. What is your will for me today?" I would do it only in 24-hour increments. But that was enough to see real progress.

At times I could not focus on anything, even God's will. That's when I discovered that I could do anything for 50 minutes that I couldn't do for 24 hours. During those occasions, I would pray for God's will, then do what I felt prompted to do for 50 minutes. I set the timer and when the alarm went off, it was time to pray and re-evaluate. This helped me stay responsive to God's will and agile enough to respond when I didn't know what else to do.

Because God answered some of my prayers really quickly, I took a step further. I bought myself the most gorgeous bound book I could find. It had pictures of happy, laughing cherubs on the front and back. This would be my miracle journal. With my Higher Power's help, I would prove to myself he was trustworthy.

I made a daily practice of recording which prayers had been answered. The amazing thing I found: He had not just answered those prayers I had written in my journal. He answered the really big prayers, the prayers for miracles and for direction in my life. What looked like setbacks and losses at the time were actually the answers to prayers.

Sometimes it was short and dramatic. My Higher Power would show up with a rather dramatic flourish. One occasion when I was desperately sad and lonely, I felt completely hollow inside. I felt so tired my heart seemed too heavy to beat.

I stood on the grounds of a very small church. It was a beautiful day. There was a bench in front of a statue of the Virgin Mary, surrounded by flowers. I'm not a Catholic, but it looked so wonderfully inviting. I sat and prayed, with tears streaming down my face, "God, I feel like no one loves me in the whole world. I need someone to love me."

As I had been praying, the preschool at the church released the kids for lunch. Dozens of adorable children ages 3-5 headed in my direction. They all wore matching red sweaters. Red is my favorite color.

A teacher asked if I minded if they hung out with me at the statue. Of course I didn't mind. They surrounded me, and a blond girl sat next to me. They began to sing *Jesus Loves Me*, and each one looked me in the eye, some with curiosity, some with love and compassion. Tears streamed down my face, as I realized my Higher Power loves me more than I can comprehend. An angel even brushed me on the shoulder with her backpack.

The tears stream down my face even now as I remember those moments. He loves me, yes he does. I began to see and recognize the times I received grace from others as I reflected on all of the times I received it from God, right there in writing. He used human foot soldiers to carry it out and, in doing so, they extended me his grace. I was training myself to see it, recognize it, and receive it.

While getting to know my Higher Power as my best friend, I went on a scriptural fast. This might not be necessary for some, but for me it was imperative. The Scriptures were part of the religion that triggered fear and blocked my view of a loving God. I didn't want anything that would trigger fear, self-judgment, or sound like more rules for me to follow perfectly or fail.

Following the same logic, I skipped church while renovating my spirit. I wanted to focus strictly on the God of here and now and be where my feet were, not in past regrets or future fears. It worked. Instead of going to Scripture, I went to God in prayer or meditation. I talked to him all through the day, as I would a friend. I took him with me everywhere I went.

One day, something amazing happened when I was hanging out with God. I heard that still, small voice within me ask, "What would you do if you weren't afraid?" Only a truly loving Higher Power who knew me better than I knew myself would ask me this.

This was the key to everything. My past. My present. And the ability to take the next step into the future simply by doing the next right thing.

Frequently I am still afraid. But asking myself this question helps me to remember all I need to do is take one step. I don't have to know where the path ultimately leads; besides, knowing where it leads does me no good.

A little too hyperactive to "meditate" in the traditional sense, I don't have a prayer mat and don't want one. I didn't want to pray in my closet. All of that called to mind subservience and submission, not surrender.

I learned to take walking meditations. When I slow down and focus on the beauty God created and focus on him, I can let go long enough to hear what he wants me to hear and see what he wants me to see.

Running meditations worked just as well. Running brought me joy, the joy made me praise God, and there he was, right with me. Musical meditations, such as singing, playing music on the guitar or piano, or even just listening, brought me such delight that I instantly praised God for the gift, and there he was, right with me.

I have lost count of how many times the answer to a specific prayer has come in the lyrics of a song. Just as often, the answer to a prayer has come in the words of a poem, formed spontaneously. The words bubble out of me like a fountain, and it is not I speaking, but he.

What I learned is, the How doesn't matter. He doesn't care how I seek him; he simply cares that I do. He is perfectly happy to tailor his communications to the way I can communicate. He knows me and knows how to speak to my heart. How he reaches me is unique and different from how he reaches someone else. How he talks with someone else is none of my business. How he talks with me is no one else's business. There is no need or room for judgment on either side. This is what having a personal relationship with God looks like.

At some point, even I had to notice the things I kept surrendering to God in my journal prayers every day were my emotions. I went from fear, to rage, to regret, to guilt, to shame, to elation, and then back to fear. But in working these three steps I learned my feelings, my thoughts, and my perceptions are not incontrovertible truth, and I learned how to manage them. I accomplished this by:

Asking "Who has the mic?" to remind myself I control the narrative of my life, and it has whatever meaning I ascribe to it. I don't have to be upset or anxious. This question also reminds me it is frequently my inner child who is distressed, not my adult self. I can listen to her, but I don't have to give her the mic.

Remembering daily, perhaps even hourly, I am writing a new story of my life, beginning today. It takes only a slight shift in direction to completely change my story and my life. It all begins with me. I see the world as I am, not necessarily as it is.

Praying immediately about whatever agitates or hurts or scares me, in order to get it out of my head and in God's hand before I have a chance to obsess or forecast disaster. It's much easier to surrender my cares and emotions minute by minute than in giant already-messed-up chunks.

I now see there had been a specific reason I thought music reached into and spoke to my soul: it did! It's God's way of helping me deal with my emotions in a spiritual way. It's God's special way of reaching my soul and calming me, without having to get mucked up in my mind. I now accept this blessing and any other he happens to throw my way.

When I'm sad, I listen to Natalie Grant's *Held* or Tenth Avenue North's *By Your Side*. If I'm thinking I'm unlovable or unloved, I listen to Mercy Me's *Beautiful*. If I'm feeling anxious and insecure about what God wants me to do, I listen to Christina Aguillera's Soar again and again. If I start to feel judged or inadequate, I rock out to Orianthi's *According to You*. It's simple, but it works for me.

The big thing I learned by journaling, working the steps, meditating, and my scriptural fast was what love is. God is love.

He is constant, soft, and yielding, not rigid and unforgiving. He shows me his boundless heart, and that reveals to me how my heart works.

In the past, I lived and worked to gain strength from my intellect. I thought my intellect was one of my major blessings. God showed me I had been focusing on the wrong organ.

True strength and safety come from living from the heart. Through my heart I could begin to feel the sorrow, sadness, and anger I had blocked with my mind for decades. This long-overdue release paved the path to freedom and the way to true humility and opened me to love.

If I attempt to follow them without regular conscious contact with God, my will, my optimism, and even—and especially—my devotion to my faith can actually be obstacles to finding and treasuring what was there all along. I don't need to search anywhere else or look to anyone else to find the answers. Both Heaven and Hell are within me; I can choose by activating the tools God had already placed within me, like discernment and wisdom.

The truth is, God is Truth. I don't have to look around every corner to find a burning bush. I just slow down and spend some time with my Higher Power, resting in him, who is Truth. I will get to the Heaven within me, if I am willing, moment-by-moment, to listen and follow. That's really all I have the power to do.

The Truth is I don't know what's good for me. Sometimes I see obstacles when they aren't really there. My perception of the end is really the beginning. I have also found again and again the worst things that ever happened to me turned out to be the best things that could ever happen to me. These things I had labeled as "bad" were loving nudges from my God in the right direction. I didn't follow, because I wanted to do the "right" thing for everyone, which is impossible. Even knowing the "right" thing for all concerned is impossible, much less acting on it.

Talk about insanity.

By way of example, I thought the second separation from my husband was the end of our family and me. It wasn't. It was kind of the beginning of a whole, new family. A better, more honest, and vulnerable family. It was the catalyst my Higher Power used to get me to slow down, focus and learn to love him, lean on him, and really know him. It was like a baptism.

The Truth is I now know integrity is not a hard, unforgiving thing, but a soft, yielding thing, like God. It's about being open, transparent, and rigorously honest in the present moment, one moment at a time, with each and every person I encounter. I work to balance my passion for honesty with kindness and compassion and the knowledge that some communications are unnecessary. It's simple, but not easy.

Finally, the last lie: being powerless before God equals being helpless and hapless. Being a "good Christian" does not require passiveness. I may be powerless to control anyone or anything, but I am not helpless. I do have power to be an advocate in my own best interest. It's not saintly or humble to abdicate this responsibility. I can make choices that are good for my health, welfare, and positive outlook. It's okay to want things, have goals, and work toward them, as long as I check in with God to see if they are aligned with his will.

Now I see. I thought this long fallow period in my life was about my Higher Power stripping things from me. But he was actually returning the most precious things to me. The things of childhood: Trust. Willingness. Surrender. Joy. Serenity. Dreams. Belief. Freedom. Abandon. Living from the Heart. That inner shimmer that comes from knowing I am loved. The ability to get out of my own light. True humility. Excitement about life simply because I'm alive. Play. Play. Play.

The only thing my Higher Power stripped from me was my grown-up illusion I had control over anything. The only thing he stripped away was my chains.

It was not about changing myself. Nor was it about removing my "defects." It was about remembering. Remembering and returning to who I really am.

BEFORE
>Spiritual Sadsack
>>Afraid of everything and everyone
>>>Heroine of victim story
>>>>Judged by everyone
>>>>>Judging everyone

AFTER
Now I can look myself in the eye every morning. I don't look all that different. I'm not suddenly famous, voluptuous, twenty years younger, or part of the cast of a sitcom. I never did win the Nobel Prize.

I haven't swapped my jeans for either Prada or sackcloth.

God never did ask me to give up all my worldly goods and move to Angola. I haven't adopted thirty children from around the world. My Higher Power asked me to do none of those things.

He asked me to remember and return, and I did.

The person I see in the mirror every day is now someone I like a lot. She's fun. She laughs and smiles. She plays. She still wants to be a Supreme... Who knows? She knows her Higher Power is not limited even by her wildest dreams.

She listens to herself. She listens to her Higher Power and treats herself with the gentleness, love, care, forgiveness, and respect her Higher Power has for her. In so doing, she has learned to trust herself and her Higher Power.

No longer does she yearn to appear strong. She has learned resilience and flexibility and the true strength that comes from letting others see her break occasionally. She is honest about her fears and shortcomings and then moves on. Still married, but marriage is not the focus of her life, identity, or spirituality. No longer a potted plant, she doesn't strain to bask in light supplied by others. She is lit from within. She has her own life, pursuits, and dreams, and has learned this isn't selfish. It is working to be in God's will. She accepts her partner as he is. She knows God will take care of her, no matter what happens.

She operates from her own convictions, not everyone else's. Her moral compass is no longer borrowed. Because she knows and likes herself, she knows her truth. If she is confused about what that truth might be in a given situation, she has ways of finding out. She knows the best way to re-connect to herself is to take time to re-connect with her Higher Power.

When necessary she speaks her truth or defends it. She has clear boundaries.

It is not impossible to have joy, peace, and love, even in trying circumstances. Even if the ones she wants love from are incapable of giving it to her right now.

This new face in the mirror is a full-grown woman. The past has been a good teacher, and it is gone.

She still worries about her kids and occasionally feels guilty for the things she couldn't do for them in the past. But she knows the best thing she can do for them is release them to the care of their own Higher Power and trust he has them in the palm of his hand.

She wakes up every morning, anticipating what will unfold and what lessons she will learn. Because she now believes in miracles, she sees them on a regular basis.

Tight with her Higher Power, she considers him a friend. She has a job she likes. She knows how to play and it refuels her. She wrote this book to help people. She writes inspirational poetry to help herself and others, and because it's just plain fun. She takes guitar lessons and plays very badly, plays the piano, writes music, all because they are just plain fun.

She enjoys hanging out with her kids because, despite all of her best efforts, they have grown to be beautiful, morally centered people, with huge, caring hearts. Somehow, they learned to live from their hearts and know who they truly are. Truth and God are her closest friends and she no longer runs from either of them.

And… yes. She sings, and sings and sings simply because it gives her joy and plugs her into all things infinite. She is at this moment practicing for her third gig with a group of women who have also come out of the fire and found spiritual freedom.

She is a work in progress and knows that will never change. She knows she's never going to "get there," wherever "there" is, and that is the point. She has found her inner child who has shown her how to play, how to be right here, right now. The words "I don't know" are no longer scary to utter. They are a call to freedom and adventure!

She is:
Redeemed
Joyous
Unencumbered
Undamned
Undimmed
Free

She knows what she labels as "bad" often turns out to be anything but. She knows what she labels as "good" sometimes turns out to be anything but. She knows there are no such things as coincidences and they are God's way of remaining anonymous. She knows his encouragement is constant and everywhere, if she is looking actively. It may not look good for a while, perhaps a long while, but it will get better. She will be taken care of. There will be enough miracles and encouragement and angels with skin on to light the way.

CHAPTER FIVE

Spiritual Toolbox
For Freedom and Recovery

Spiritual Toolbox For Freedom and Recovery

I leave to you to determine if the steps and tools I've outlined here are worth pursuing, but for me they are the difference between "Before" and "After." They look simple but are not particularly easy at first. The results can be gratifying and dramatic. Take what you like and whatever works for you.

CHAPTER 5 🌣 *Spiritual Toolbox For Freedom and Recovery*

What follows are thumbnail descriptions of some of the tools I discovered during my escape from the Old Testament and subsequent recovery, as discussed in much more detail elsewhere. This is a ready cheat sheet of things that have worked for me.

#1. Whenever and wherever necessary, fire any vengeful God that withholds love and forgiveness. Replace with a loving Higher Power who wants your freedom and happiness.

#2. Fire any Old Testament talking heads who spout Old Testament judgments. Adopt the view that there are two experts on your life: God and you. Period.

#3. Pray for God's will.

#4. Ask for confirmation.

#5. Detach. Let it go. All of it, including yourself. Everything but prayer and your Higher Power's will.

#6. After receiving confirmation of his will, ask, "What would you do if you weren't afraid?" and go do it!

#7. Boldly ask for what you want and need from God, no matter how great or small. It's up to him to say yes or no. There is no need to judge yourself for merely asking.

#8. Wait.

#9. Rest. Sometimes pushing ahead or "toughing it out" are not virtues. They can lead to spiritual confusion, physical exhaustion, and wrong decisions.

#10. Meditate. Meditating, resting and waiting are not doing nothing. They are hanging out with God and giving us the opportunity to more fully know his will and his character, which will strengthen us and make us more confident in our actions and decisions.

#11. Work "recovery steps" one, two and three.
   a) Admit you are powerless, not helpless. There is a difference. Explore the difference.
   b) Believe you can and will be restored to your former self.
   c) Make a decision to surrender to his care. Decide to trust him.

#12. When in doubt, repeat all of the above steps. When confused, repeat the above steps. When lonely, despondent, resentful, angry, or afraid, repeat the above steps. Repeat... until you can really trust in a loving spiritual parent who asks only your willingness to grow and follow his will. Keep repeating until you learn to trust yourself in this process and trust God is in you. This is a lifestyle choice, not a crash diet.

#13. Banish perfection in all aspects of life and replace it with willingness as your standard.

#14. Adopt the belief that the Truth is always your friend and God is Truth itself.

#15. Adopt the belief that there are no coincidences, and see how many of your prayers <u>God answers</u> in this way.

#16. Ask for miracles and keep a miracle journal. This turned out to be the most life-giving thing I could do for myself. Once I started recording my prayers and how often they were answered, I began to see my Higher Power's unconditional love for me.

#17. Conceive of and believe the idea that God never wastes a hurt. If something is painful now, it may be because the foundation is being laid for some seismic change. We have only a minuscule view of the whole scenario.

#18. Find and cultivate the "people" who are your sanctuary. Your "people" are those who want and accept the truth from and about you, no matter what, because they want you to heal and grow. They are not in the judging business. They can be at Church or at the gym or at Taco Bell. Chances are, you already know who they are.

#19. It's easier and more productive to do a daily inventory of things that went well and things you would like to improve upon and then let it go, than to ask forgiveness for regrets years later. Consider it good spiritual hygiene.

#20. Finally, if it seems there is no love in your life, or you are giving love and care but not receiving what you need, love yourself as a loving God would. Treat yourself with the compassion, gentleness, forgiveness, and respect your Higher Power would accord you.

Some of these concepts merit further explanation
Prayer is an active verb. So is waiting. Prayer can be a tonic, a cure, a cry, a thank-you, or all of the above. It can be silent, trusting God to know what is heavy on my heart. Often, it is the only thing I can do. But it sets things into motion and calls things into being. It unleashes the power of God and brings it into the person, situation, or other matter about which I am praying.

I pray about some matters as soon as I am aware of them. With my ADHD, if I wait until a formal "prayer time," I will likely forget what it was I wanted to bring to God. Even worse, if I have fears or resentments, I have found it is best to give them to God immediately before they have a chance to burrow their way into my thinking and my heart.

Waiting is also significant in and of itself. It means something. I am doing something when I wait: I am giving my Higher Power time to act on my behalf and perhaps even provide a miracle or answer a prayer. As I wait, I ask myself, *What is the gift in this situation?* Then I pray. Waiting also helps me trust myself and the voice of God within me telling me things aren't ready for me yet.

Ask. This has to do with prayer. For the longest time, I didn't believe I had the right to ask God for "good" things, so I never asked, and believed I never received. Today, I ask him for what I need, but it's okay to ask him for what I want, too. If I'm scared, I ask him to take my fear. If I'm worried about my child or myself, I ask that he take care of and protect us. I ask him to take my character defects. I ask him to repair broken relationships.

My point is: I've stopped being a Prayer Editor. No request is too trivial, stupid, or selfish. If I simply ask for whatever is on my heart, it helps me detach from final outcomes and trust the right thing will happen. I back up and let God be God. I let him decide which prayers he will answer with a yes. I ask for his will in my life and let him decide what that is and show me.

Because subtlety is a foreign language for me, I ask him to show me his will clearly. Because I am strong-willed and can tend to think my will and his will are the same, I ask again for confirmation of what I think his will is any time my direction seems to be changing.

The Enemy

Resistance is the enemy. The biggest obstacle to using any of these tools successfully is resistance, or the lack of detachment. Detachment is essential, and it is quite a complex beast, but no true recovery can happen without it.

The hardest part for me was surrender and detachment along with realizing the two go hand in hand. God's will was the flow of a current, not a hammer coming down on my head or a tornado that would remove me from one place and put me in another. I learned to overcome my resistance to this flow. To do this, I detached from everything but my Higher Power's will for me.

The only way I can do it is hit my knees every morning and ask for his will only for the day. Sometimes I have to ask for it in 30-minute increments.

It's the most difficult step I've ever taken in my own best interest. It means detachment from fixing/meddling with/ controlling/making demands of other people, their emotions, goals, and problems. Even my children and spouse. *Especially* my children and spouse. If I am hovering like a helicopter, trying to ensure they won't be hurt, I am making myself a human shield between them and their own Higher Power, who has a better plan for them than I could ever dream. Letting go of my loved ones' outcomes, emotions and problems will allow me to focus on myself, my Higher Power, and to zero in on his/ her will for me. That's all I really have power to do, anyway.

I detached from my emotional tendency to live in the past and the future. Being an artistic, passionate sort, I get my fuel from my emotions. They are a huge part of my identity and my productivity. But feelings are not facts.

I have to work on letting go of my story, my need to rewrite it, and my need for justice. The only way I could do that, frankly, was to tell it here. Then I saw it in perspective. I saw that I had a part in the things that happened, and that part was large. I was not a victim, after all. I healed from the wrongs and the hurts and finally saw it as in the past.

When I trust that my Higher Power's got me and his plan is better than mine, I take my hands off of outcomes and expectations. I detach from both kinds of illusions: those of power, and those of helplessness. Both are equally destructive. Both will lead me further and further from the truth.

If I believe I have power over people, places, and things, power that really belongs to God, I stall on my path while I wrestle and struggle with his will. I become exhausted and negative and frustrated, while my faith and trust diminish.

If I go the other way and believe I'm helpless, I'm expecting God to do what I could be doing. I'm going to end up in the same place: stalled, frustrated, and losing faith. Before God can show up for me, I simply have to show up for myself. There is no way to get on the right path without taking a step or two of my own volition.

Inextricably intertwined in this critical process is detachment from one's religious affiliation

I don't mean become an atheist. I mean step far enough back

from the rituals, the policies, and the politics of one's church to see and hear God, so you can realize religion is populated by fallible humans just like you, who might occasionally be wrong or not know the whole story. They can easily become idols while we are not paying attention, leading us farther from our path and the truth.

I don't mean physical detachment either, as in staying away. I mean emotional detachment.

This is critical. Just as I can tell myself stories about me and others that aren't true, I can tell myself stories about God and what he wants for me that aren't true. If I focus on my Higher Power and on my desire to know him and his will for me, I will be much less susceptible to judgment from others. I will also be less likely to let a need for approval provoke me to supplant the will of religious figures or even peers for God's, or their opinions for what I know to be true in my heart.

How to accomplish this detachment? Practice the tools discussed herein. Read and repeat the Scriptures discussed below, or ones you prefer. Go on your own Bible Discovery Mission and find the verses that seem to speak directly to your heart and reassure you that your God really knows you. Download a Bible application to your phone or tablet and have those verses ready any time you may be doubtful, weary or afraid. Stop fear in its tracks. Pray for what you need and refer to your ready scriptures that calm and comfort you or give you courage.

And one more thing: Mind your own business. What others think of you, even if they are important or "holy," has nothing to do with your path and is only a distraction. They are entitled to think what they want, and it has nothing to do with your life. If I'm focused on others and their opinions, I'm not living my life; I'm living theirs. In the same vein, what I may think of someone else's behavior, choices, motivations, or even how they treat me is not my business to manage. I have no way of knowing what the facts are. It's simply a distraction that takes my eyes and ears off of God.

Have a scriptural toolbox that isn't borrowed from someone else

Just as I could use the Bible and its words to club myself, I could take a more discerning look and choose to rest in those Scriptures that affirmed what I believed my Higher Power wanted for and from me.

The Bible says something different to everyone who reads it, and that is why it is a living, breathing testament of our Higher Power's presence in our lives. I get to decide what he wants it to mean for me, with his confirmation. These are discussed in much more detail elsewhere, but these work for me most of the time.

They replaced my cage walls with the four walls of a temple of sorts within which I can rest and remember I, too, am the sacred creation of my creator.

> *Above all else, guard your heart for it is the wellspring of life.*[23]

I can't fix my mind with my mind. I have to live from the heart to be who God wants me to be.

> *The Kingdom of God is within you.*[24]

I don't have to wait until heaven to be happy or free. If the kingdom is within me, then I already have everything I need within me. I just need to excavate it.

> *Though the mountains be shaken and the hills be removed, yet my unfailing love for you will not be shaken nor my covenant of peace be removed...*[25]

I can trust a God who loves me this much. He only wants good things for me. That's really all there is to it.

> *Put on the full armor of God, so that when the day of evil comes, you may be able to stand your ground, and after you have done everything, to stand. Stand firm then, with the belt of truth buckled around your waist, with the breastplate of righteousness in place, and with your feet fitted with the readiness that comes from the gospel of peace. In addition... take up your shield of faith... the helmet of salvation and the sword of the Spirit, which is the word of God. And pray in the spirit on all occasions all kinds of prayers and requests.*[26]

We can put on God's protection any time we want to and take it with us everywhere we go. Our strength is to stand with God, as he stands with us. We are never alone.

> *Therefore, my dear friends, flee from idolatry. I speak to sensible people; judge for yourselves what I say.*[27]

We need no intermediary or interpreter to speak to or hear from God or to speak for ourselves.

Take these if you like them, or throw them out and find the

ones that seem to work for you. Everyone gets to go on this journey of discovery and find the words that most speak to him or her. It is a life-long spiritual adventure.

Finally, if I am feeling really far from God because I am mourning a loss, nursing resentment or am feeling alone, I give myself the gift of perspective and time. I remember all of the other times that I felt the same way and I cried out to God and he answered in the most beautiful and personal ways. I remember my own personal band of angels, clothed in red sweaters, singing Jesus Loves Me. I remember all of the "losses" I experienced in the past that turned out to be time-outs to allow my Higher Power to set the stage for an opportunity, a blessing or even a miracle.

CHAPTER SIX

Idols, A Remix

I overheard a conversation recently which was life changing for me.

The man whom I was pretending not to overhear was saying the word integrity simply meant undiminished. Joy-undiminished. Enthusiasm-undiminished. Personality-undiminished.

Beautiful. It was what I had unsuccessfully tried to articulate my whole life in my faith. Of what use am I to God if I am not being my authentic self?

Faith and finding one's spiritual destiny is not about following the rules; it's about realizing the rules do not define who I am, owning and loving who I really am, and preserving and protecting her. Can I face and participate with my pastor/ my friends /my community and give of myself without abandoning myself to these groups?

Now, I can happily say yes. I no longer let other people or a set of rules define who I am. I no longer try to serve in every arena simply because that way I will disappoint no one. I no longer apologize for or explain myself. If God made me who I am, why would I try to subtract from his work?

When people of faith place too much trust in rules, rigid doctrines, or well-intentioned leaders with feet of clay, they and we can get hurt. There can be a lot of collateral damage. Spiritual paths get diverted, identities get misplaced, and unlikely idols get created.

Can a doctrine be an idol? Can a church be an idol? Can a pastor be an idol? Can even the Bible be an idol, if used to denigrate and deny our fellow creations? If we use the Bible to turn our backs on certain segments of humanity, who or what are we worshipping, really? I learned coming into contact with a faith community is a test of one's own spiritual integrity, and not in the most obvious sense.

Golden Calves
So, can the Bible or a church be an idol?

In my experience, the answer is yes, if circumstances cause us to leave our true selves in the collection plate.

Am I saying that every person who sacrifices to live his or her life as a pastor sets himself or herself up as an idol? Definitely not.

But I believe we should go directly to our Higher Power for answers first, before seeking an intermediary, because we want to avoid making that person our idol. Many people hear from their own churches or their pastors a particular message about whom God is urging them to become, but find themselves contradicting or fighting it, and then judged for following their own hearts. This seems particularly true for women in the churches I attended on my pilgrimage.

I told my own story, but I've also seen it at work in other people's lives. The conflict can be subtle. An artist friend of mine was repeatedly encouraged to embrace leadership at her church and was told it was her path. She had no interest in this area and believed she could lead others through her art more effectively than becoming part of the church hierarchy. She wasn't told she was wrong. There simply was never an artistic avenue given to her to lead, and no church leaders were ever available to discuss what she believed her path to be. She left

CHAPTER 6 ❦ *Idols, A Remix* 149

the church and developed a strong, devoted following. Once it was clear that she was famous, at least locally, she was invited by that same church to return and lead with her artistic talent.

In another instance, a friend of mine with a real interest and talent for leadership wanted to get involved in leadership of her church. She had been a leader in both her professional and personal lives for most of her seventy years. She had been one of her pastor's right-hand people. She felt her church of twenty years was taking a dangerous direction and needed a major course correction. She sent an e-mail to her pastor summarizing her concerns and indicating her willingness to become involved in creating the solution. She never got a meeting with him or a response to the e-mail. She tried going through his assistant and through other channels. In whatever capacity they would have her, she offered to assist or lead. It was as if she ceased to exist. When she attempted to follow up on her many requests in person, the reception was decidedly cold, or bewildered as to what she was talking about. She had no alternative but to leave her church of twenty years, and to my knowledge, has not set foot in another church.

I found I could only enter into a personal relationship with God one on one. A community of believers can amplify this relationship and enhance the relationship but cannot stand in its place. The sermons can provide insight, answers, and teachings that further stimulate our quest to know God better.

We can find community. By helping those who need it most, we can reach out together to help our cities, states, and country. This is an essential function of the church.

But church can't tell us who we were created to be.
No church can judge us.
Only God can judge us.

No one can do the heavy lifting for us, and if we rely on others to do it, aren't we diminishing ourselves and making idols of them? Aren't we becoming less ourselves, as we hasten to God's call on their lives instead of his call on our own?

It's about whom I am out of church and in the world that matters and whether that person is the same person in and out of the church building. Can I be the true me, undimmed, undiminished in all my interactions, even with church elders and Bible scholars?

Yes, if I am doing my own spiritual work and, through it, have discovered my spiritual self. Once I realized I had a choice between viewing my spirituality and all things flowing from it as infinite and inclusive, instead of rigid and exclusive, I opened up to a whole new world, previously unseen. I could have this kind of spirituality and my Christian faith at the same time. Once I realized that God could call me in an infinite variety of ways, I truly embraced the infinite possibilities for being on my true path. I can't miss it, if I am seeking God's will. A gargantuan weight of anxiety dropped off of my shoulders. I can be anything and anywhere God wants me to be at any time. I am not limited by only the possibilities that I can see. Others have no power to influence my relationship with God or my path by what they perceive, what they say or what they see.

In The Beginning Was The… Soundbite?
If I go to McChurch expecting detailed, personalized, and

CHAPTER 6 ❦ *Idols, A Remix*

intimate spiritual revelations, don't I kind of deserve what I get? The only person who can truly interpret what any given scripture or doctrine means to me is me.

It's a solitary road God and I walk. Anyone else's interpretation of what it means for my life may be accurate or it may be just another point of view, colored by personal experience and bias. If I consistently defer to anyone else's interpretation, aren't I just idolizing both the point of view and the speaker? How can I inspire or help anyone if I am walking someone else's spiritual path? While I strain to hear what someone else thinks those instructions are, I may miss my very specific guidance from God. If I treat the Scriptures any other way, aren't I completely at odds with what Jesus said and did?

> *And no one puts new wine into old wineskins. If he does, the wine will burst the skins, and both the wine and the wineskins will be ruined. No, he pours new wine into new wineskins.*[28]

The presence of the Kingdom of God requires new and surprising ways for him to express his will. If I am truly open to God's ability to work in me, I have to be open to, look for and even welcome unexpected surprises and messages. If I cling to the burning bush or someone else's message, I might be throwing out the "new wine" of God's Kingdom.[29]

If I am a one-of-a-kind work created by God, then won't his guidance and instructions for me be a new work, too? Won't they be tailored for me as I read and receive them?

If we think God needs an interpreter, aren't we saying he has limited ability to communicate effectively?

> *So is my word that goes out of my mouth: It will not return to me empty, but will accomplish what I desire and achieve the purpose for which I sent it.*[30]

It doesn't sound to me like God needs our help speaking for him. The same scriptures can give new revelation even now. In fact, the same scripture can reveal different things at different times and to different people. If viewed as static and immutable instead of dynamic and living, the scriptures themselves can serve as an idol.

God did not stop talking when Paul finished his letters to the Galatians, or Thessalonians or Corinthians, or when the other Apostles finished their accounts of Jesus and his life. There is nothing finite about God or his word.

Seeing With Cataracts

There are a lot of people out there like me: former addicts of one kind or another, women in crisis and in pain. We are looking for answers and to be part of something bigger. We are all looking for God with skin on at one time or another.

The good news is that now we can reach thousands of people in church and millions more in the media and the Internet. The bad news is there is no way to cover it all instantly or even quickly; the beauty and the subtlety of all the many levels of meaning in the Bible.

This can only be an introduction that causes a hunger to

delve into God and his word in more detail.

The danger is that religion isn't God. It's an idol, if we worship it in and of itself, and for some of us it is hard to make the distinction. It can become a Golden Calf, just like the one the Israelites worshipped. While Moses stood with God on Mount Sinai receiving the Ten Commandments, his people became restless. They approached Aaron and said, *Come, make us gods who will go before us. As for this fellow Moses who brought us out of Egypt, we don't know what has happened to him.*[31]

Aaron instructed them to remove their gold jewelry and give it to him. He took the gold, melted it, and fashioned it into an idol cast in the shape of a calf. Then they said, *These are your gods, Israel, who brought you up out of Egypt.*[32]

Aaron then erected an altar in front of the calf and the next day the people gave sacrifices to the idol. Moses returned from the mountain to view this spectacle and, in his anger, threw down the tablets containing the Ten Commandments, and broke them. Moses then asked those who were still loyal to the Lord to come and go with him. He instructed these loyal men to slay their fellow Jews. The ones who strayed momentarily lost their focus because of fear and doubt and ultimately lost everything.

Religion can cause us to shift our focus from God, the Source of everything, just long enough to become an idol. Before we know it, with the best of intentions, we have erected it and are kneeling before it. We knelt before God, but somehow we are now kneeling before something else entirely.

Ritual. Fear. Fellowship. Legalism. This can happen so easily if we don't know who we are spiritually when we walk into church.

We always have to keep in mind that our God is with us and in us. Our church is not our God. God is not the church or its leaders, or even its doctrines. We are carrying the armor of God with us. The armor of God is his word in the Bible, his direct communications with us and his holy spirit, who is with us always.

We put on his righteousness and truth and carry it with us. We can put on his peace and carry it with us. We carry the sword of the spirit with us.[33] When we carry these items with us, we will be teachable by God and not malleable by man. We will not be ruled by man's praise or rejection. We will have what we need to withstand these pressures.

The rest of the scripture is instructive:

> *...so you may be able to stand your ground, and after you have done everything, to stand. Stand firm then, with the belt of truth buckled around your waist, with the breastplate of righteousness in place, and with your feet fitted with the readiness that comes from the gospel of peace. In addition to all of this, take up the shield of faith, with which you can extinguish all the flaming arrows of the evil one. Take the helmet of salvation and the sword of the Spirit, which is the word of God. And pray in the Spirit on all occasions with all kinds of prayers and requests.*[34]

We are told to stand two times in this brief scripture for a reason, I think.

Everything we need, we already have, if we have done our spiritual work. For then we know the character of God. We know he is always for us and always with us. Who we are isn't wrong. We have the confidence and assurance produced in an ongoing relationship with God, and therefore we see and know how God communicates with us individually. Knowing this, we are more apt to see the difference between our path and someone else's.

A human organization can only shrink God, because man cannot perceive the vastness of God. Yes, God created the Church to be his bride. But each church is peopled by more people just like me, just like you, whom God created to be fallible and have free will.

> *Please, God do away with all the men and women who belittle you, Infatuated with cheap God imitations...*[35]

But the church isn't our only avenue of revelation. God did not stop talking in Jesus' time. He did not lose the ability to talk to us. He is not imprisoned in the Bible. He can use it if he wants. He can communicate directly with us anytime through any method or medium. He is God, after all.

When contemplation and study of the words of the Bible becomes a rigid adherence to the exact words as rules to be followed, regardless of the context of when they were written or who reads them, might we then be worshipping the words? To be certain, we will be judged by our actions. But that judgment will come from God who knows our hearts as well.

When a human organization trains its focus on actions instead of the heart, everything gets warped. People can be judged based on perceptions instead of reality.

A culture of enforcement can inadvertently be created. Behaviors are either encouraged or discouraged, instead of belief being fostered and nurtured.

Surrender can become submission.

Community can become conformity.

Acceptance can become resignation.

Hope can become fear.

Repentance can become shame, and from shame, it isn't a big leap to blame.

Words are sacred, but not static. They are alive and have all the power and meanings that God does. They will mean something to me unique and different from what they mean to you. As in the scripture, they, and Christ, have been with us since the beginning.[35] He truly knows us and knows how to speak to us.

He knows what words, and which interpretation of those words to use. That is part of a personal relationship with God. If we treat the scriptures in any other way, aren't we at odds with what Jesus said and did?

The word of God is the antithesis of a one size fits all anything.

Could it be idolatry to use God's words to denigrate or humiliate one of his creations? I believe so, because every human creation houses the divine.

> *Teacher, which is the greatest commandment in the Law?*
> *Jesus replied: 'Love the lord... with all your heart... and the second is like it:*
> *'Love your neighbor as yourself.'* [36]

If a person's heart doesn't matter, then we are all condemned and damned. This has even greater repercussions: if only our actions can be judged, then we are all either the judged or the accusers. We are all either Pharisees or Lepers.

Which side would you rather be on?

Fear short-circuits the lifecycle of faith:

1) Acceptance of self
2) Surrender of self
3) Humility
4) Receipt of grace from God and others
5) And, finally, Transformation

If we fear consequences for not conforming, aren't we sinning or falling short of the mark God intended for us?

The Bible talks about fear a lot and in only one place is fear called a good thing. That one good fear is Fear of the Lord.

> *...save your fear for God, who holds your entire life— body and soul—in his hands.* [37]

Fear creates human cyclones of shame and blame.

If I don't love or accept myself, I have the option of judging myself. If I judge myself, I might feel unworthy for never measuring up to my own standards or those of others.

If I feel unworthy and judgment is the only tool in my toolbox, I will project these feelings of unworthiness on everyone else, judging them as I judge myself.

The only fear that doesn't inhibit true positive transformation is reverential fear of the Lord. Fear prevents an authentic transformation from occurring because it short-circuits the process from even starting. Not only does it prevent surrender from occurring, because of fear of exposure and judgment or punishment; fear prevents acceptance of self from occurring.

If seeing my sins causes me to shrink back into denial rather than having to confess them and risk shame, it's going to be that much more difficult to face myself. If I haven't yet faced and accepted my true self, how will I love myself? If I don't love myself, how much more difficult it will be to believe God sees me as loveable.

One step builds upon another. They follow a sequence.

There is no fear in love... Perfect love drives out fear, because fear has to do with punishment...[38]

Jesus was not afraid to break the rules. He healed on the Sabbath. He intervened and ultimately prevented the stoning of an adulterous woman, which was the law at the time. He spent his time with those his society deemed " bad people." He overthrew the tables of the moneychangers, challenging and chastising the power-base of his society.

If anyone says, 'I love God,' yet hates his brother, he is a liar. For anyone who does not love his brother, whom

he has seen, cannot love God, whom he has not seen.[39]
The scriptures have a lot to say about the danger of idols.

Of what value is an idol, since a man has carved it? Or an image that teaches lies? For he who makes it trusts in his own creation; he makes idols that cannot speak.[40]

> *Those who cling to worthless idols, forfeit grace that could be theirs.*[41]

You shall have no other Gods before me.[42]

If I go to a person first, any person, before I go to God in prayer and meditation for answers, am I making of that human being an idol? These scriptures lead me to believe, in some instances that may be the case. That is what I did in my early life and God gently tried to bring that to my attention. I disrespected him by going to the wrong place for truth, love, and answers.

> *For it is written; I will destroy the wisdom of the wise; the intelligence of the intelligent, I will frustrate.*[43]

> *...God was pleased through the foolishness of what was preached to save those who believe...*[44]

> *The fear of the Lord is the beginning of wisdom; all who follow his precepts have good understanding.*[45]

All of this leads me to an even greater "what if?"

What if, in evangelizing and outreach with the best of intentions, we have placed ourselves in the role of religious idols?

What if, in our haste to share our own personal truth with seekers or fellow believers, we are robbing them of theirs? What if we are violating them?

What if, in our efforts to be heard by them and reach them, we stop seeing them? What if, in our efforts to help them see God in us, we rob them of the opportunity to see God in themselves or see God himself?

What if we are spiritually hobbling ourselves, and by extension, those we are trying to reach, by not allowing them the chance to heal?

How can we read the scriptures about God's word and believe all God has to say is entombed in a 2000-year-old book? It is sacred and it is God, but it is only a part of him. What if we are literally cutting him off mid-sentence?

If we think he needs us to interpret or speak for him, isn't that arrogant, and again putting ourselves in the role of a big, shiny Golden Calf?

And finally, a word about wisdom:

Wisdom is part of a lifetime spent trying to discern and do God's will. It is not hurried and does not bow to pressure. It is a product of spiritual maturity. Wisdom most definitely can be found at church, in nature, or spoken out of the mouths of our children, wherever and however God chooses to impart it.

All I am saying is, shouldn't we go to the source of all wisdom, strength, courage and love first? Shouldn't we put on the full armor of God, before we go anywhere, even church?

We simply cannot know all there is to know about God or

any human. It is unknowable, because we can't see with the eyes of God or know with the mind of God.

God, and his word have been likened to a diamond, with more facets than can be counted with the naked eye.[46] The infinite gem looks completely different depending on the light and the angle.

If this is true of God, and we are created in God's image, then isn't it also true of us?

What mortal man can judge? Won't each of us appear different according to that which is brought to light and that which has yet to be exposed?

If we are all as precious, as resplendent and as flawed as a diamond, what possible purpose can there be to hurrying the cutting process? Hurrying it may result in only dust.

The meekest, the weakest, those with the least faith or reason for faith may eventually burn the brightest if given the chance. They have a story to tell. They're not finished talking yet either. All they need is mercy and time to grow and be transformed how and when God wants to accomplish that. He wants to do a new thing in and for them and us.

CHAPTER SEVEN

Upside Down Faith

CHAPTER 7 ❦ *Upside Down Faith*

Codependency is the daily, hourly practice of idolatry. Codependents have had their faith turned upside down. Their faith is inverted because they unintentionally worship human beings instead of God.

Codependency takes religious teachings and ideas and sets them on their ear. People who are merely exercising authority in their own lives suddenly have authority in our lives. We give it to them rather than alienate them by asserting a boundary, because we think we need their approval or because we lack a sense of self and are trying to find worth.

What happens at the intersection of the Codependent and her religion? What happens to her when she collides with a McChurch and a culture of enforced conformity? Can she surrender and transform? How does she? What happens to faith? What happens to her?

The Codependent leads a life that can spiral from fear to shame and back again. Love of self is often not an option. Peace is not an option, because that comes from self-acceptance.

Joy is not an option because it has been replaced by duty, service and earning esteem. Many of these people don't know how to recognize grace or give it. Self-acceptance may feel like a sin. True love and acceptance of fellow humans can't occur, because it is blocked by fear they will judge, disapprove or reject.

How can true transformation occur in this pressure cooker?

God has either totally disappeared or is irrelevant at this point.

It's a dysfunctional family on steroids. Normal is as remote and incomprehensible as quantum physics.

Codependency has been linked to abusive or dysfunctional behavior from family caregivers, and, in 2009, 3.3 million child abuse reports were made affecting an estimated six million children.[47] We can safely assume there are at least as many Codependents in our houses of worship as in the general population. This is a very significant portion of the body of Christ! These dysfunction refugees are not "out there" to be visited on a mission trip. They are sitting in our pews.

Imagine the ramifications.

How do you send a message of redemption, forgiveness, and transformation to someone whose go-to responses are shame and fear?

> *The important thing is not to stop questioning.*
> ~ Albert Einstein

My focus in this chapter is on these narrow issues and my approach is spiritual instead of clinical. My references to Codependents refer to those who are untreated or not yet in a recovery program. Volumes have been written on the subject of Codependency, its clinical symptoms, and treatment, and in these pages I cannot improve upon what is already there. Some of the foremost authorities on this subject are Pia Mellody, Keith Miller, and Andrea Wells Miller.

In their masterpiece, *Facing Codependence*, the authors distinguish Codependents from others by stating that Codependents experience esteem from others instead of experiencing their own internal value and esteem as human beings.[48]

A characteristic of Codependency is carried shame, which produces and reproduces feelings of worthlessness.[49] Carried shame is shame without an appropriate cause. A person experiencing this is ashamed for being, not for anything they have actually done. She might:

1. Have low self-esteem.
2. Experience a great deal of difficulty setting boundaries.
3. Have difficulty distinguishing between her own experience and feelings and those of others.
4. Have difficulty taking care of her needs and wants.
5. Have difficulty expressing her own reality and experiences moderately.[50]

For the most part, this list describes difficulty distinguishing one's self from others. When someone who is ashamed of simply being hears teachings about humility, church sermons can do real damage. Someone in this mindset has a beaten-down ego and can't distinguish between humility and humiliation. She esteems the words of others more than her own, making her vulnerable to teachings from authority figures, whether those teachings help or hurt her.

As a former raging codependent, I know how the thinking goes: I earn love by being good. I earn respect and approval by being good. Being good means meeting everyone else's needs and not causing trouble. Selfishness is not acceptable. Having a self is selfish. If I work hard, I can get my needs met. If they aren't being met, I'll work harder.

Working hard can mean putting myself beneath others and their goals, because I don't know what I really want or need or how to get it yet. If I can serve others, I can control or at least influence their behavior. I can create rigid rules for myself in an attempt to be perfect. All because of fear. I fear discovery, because then others might see my imperfection and unworthiness and shame me for it. I fear surrender because I've already surrendered my self to others. What is left to surrender to a higher power?

If a parent does not allow children to learn to make some decisions for themselves, the children never go through the developmental process in which they learn to feel good about doing things their own way. If this micro-managing is carried to the extreme to what the children are allowed to believe, they lose touch of what their own way is. Such children have to wait for other people to tell them how to do almost any new thing, even as *adults*. This is one of the definitions of spiritual abuse.[51]

These children are stripped of the ability to form into unique and mature spiritual beings. Those who have experienced it can be primed to be and stay in spiritually uncomfortable or abusive situations because they feel familiar and don't know escape is an option.

This is the culture of enforcement discussed previously, but it is self-imposed!

These refugees often need rigid rules to feel safe. They look for a church or a mate to fill this requirement.

We can understand the initial attraction of a Codependent to the formality, the structure and predictability and rules of church. Looks like a match made in heaven. Often besieged by guilt and feelings of unworthiness, because she can't ever meet everyone else's needs, she finds an opportunity to really contribute.

Sometimes, it really is a match made in heaven. But, often, propriety and the need for acceptance and approval can block any truly authentic spiritual encounter. Church can become an exclusive club to get in and staying in can become the number one goal. The gospel becomes an entrance exam and nothing more. The joy and peace resulting from a true and deep understanding of the gospel never arrives.

It is a real challenge for any church of any size to recognize this fragile group, because they are often such model church citizens. They love to serve. They give of their time, talents, and finances, sometimes until it hurts a lot.

My hope is maybe more churches will begin to recognize them as the dysfunction refugees they are, instead of seeing them merely as extremely committed volunteers and the solution to a manpower problem.

But, in the meantime, what is the solution for the religious Codependent?

A large part of the answer is freedom. The outgrowth of complete reliance on and trust in God is the freedom from fear of other humans. The freedom described in the twenty-seventh Psalm. Easier said than done, but this is a pretty good roadmap of how to get there:

The Lord is my light and salvation; whom shall I fear?

The Lord is the stronghold of my life; of whom shall I be afraid? When evildoers assail me to eat up my flesh, my adversaries and foes, it is they who stumble and fall. Though an army encamp against me, my heart shall not fear... yet I will be confident... He will hide me in his shelter in the day of trouble; and he will lift me high upon a rock... For my mother and father have forsaken me, but the Lord will take me in... Give me not up to the will of my adversaries.[52]

This whole Psalm is about God versus other human beings. God is with the Psalmist against his enemies. He has no fear because he is aligned with God and trusts him, not watching what his enemies do. He has confidence he will prevail over those who mean him harm because he knows he has divine protection.

Most importantly the Psalmist has autonomy, something many Codependents have difficulty embracing. He has his light and salvation and needs nothing and no one else. He is not subject to any human's will. His focus is on his heavenly father.

The enemies described in the Psalm do not just refer to outer things, but inner things as well. The Psalmist's own fears come from within and assail him to eat up his flesh. What a perfect description of the destructive inner war our fears wage.

For a Codependent who isn't centered in her Higher Power, her heart can be a roiling cauldron of fear, shame, and resentment. The remedy is freedom from this stronghold.

Freedom to question any person, to recognize hurtful influences and step back from them, to decide for oneself what is best and what to believe. But this freedom must be learned and practiced until she feels it is part of her and can exercise it at will. That might take a while. It might take a sabbatical away from authority figures and opportunities to earn approval and esteem.

The basic minimum requirement for a loving, if not perfectly functional, family is acceptance. For those who didn't find this growing up, it is so important to find it in our spiritual community.

But acceptance by others can't occur before acceptance of self. But, first there must be a self to accept. That is the hardest step and may take the longest, as my lengthy spiritual pilgrimage illustrates.

When I finally found the right spiritual home for my family and me, it was like the escape scene from *The Shawshank Redemption*. The hero escapes prison through a series of sewer tunnels, and once freed, gulps the sweet, clean air, and pauses to joyfully take it in. I could breathe deeply, feeling I was safe in the arms of family. I didn't have to earn acceptance or anything else here. No matter how long it took, it was worth it. I lost everything for a time, but I got myself back.

For we Codependents, it is imperative that the loving spiritual family waits until we discover ourselves and learn to be spiritual, yet autonomous. First, we must experience our brokenness and imperfection as *fearfully* and *wonderfully made*[53] by our Creator and not as items to be fixed or hidden, or to earn acceptance. Then and only then will we have the ability to be part of a faith community without being absorbed and erased by it.

This freedom and autonomy may only arrive after a separation from the things that are triggers to approval-seeking and subjugation of our views and feelings to those of others. A spiritual road trip described in chapter 4 could be really beneficial before going to church. Ideally, we should be spiritually autonomous enough to ask questions, protect our boundaries, and evaluate our experiences as desirable or undesirable before seeking to merge with a larger spiritual community. Ironically, the remedy for fear of others' disapproval and rejection may be experiencing being alone and discovering there is nothing to fear in that. There is nothing to fear in being without human company or approval because we discover we are not alone at all! We begin the most magnificent relationship of our lives.

> *So do not fear, for I am with you; do not be dismayed, for I am your God. I will strengthen you and help you; I will uphold you with my righteous right hand... Though you search for your enemies, you will not find them. Those who wage war against you will be nothing at all. For I am the Lord, your God, who takes hold of your right hand and says to you, Do not fear; I will help you.*[54]

After we discover who we are isn't wrong or less than any other mortal man, finding and joining a spiritual family that allows us to contribute as equals will be more likely, because we accept and love ourselves. Once we learn we are worth loving, protecting, and defending simply because God made us, we can fortify ourselves against those who would run over us or force us to conform.

We have a right and a reason to be here. God made us for himself to enjoy, and there is no higher purpose!

> *For you created my inmost being; you knit me together in my mother's womb. I praise you, because I am fearfully and wonderfully made; your works are wonderful. I know it full well.*[55]

CONCLUSION

(The Real Good News)

CONCLUSION *(The Real Good News)*

Clean your finger before you point out my spots.
~ Benjamin Franklin

CONCLUSION ❦ *(The Real Good News)* 179

No Dogma

In my attempts to "master" meditation, I listened to a lot of "Meditation Music" designed to assist in this process. I stumbled upon a little song called " Fireflies" that consistently transported me to that meditative state during its two-minute duration, when nothing else worked.[56]

It was a little miracle. Its simple, swirling melody perfectly evoked darting fireflies at twilight chased by my laughing brothers and me. Happy childhood memories, tears of joy, and the feeling of being able to communicate with God flooded that two-minute space.

Within two days, I wanted to capture that melody and make it mine. I sat down at the piano and began to pick out the notes to the song. To my immense irritation, I found it was simple. That knowledge changed the power the song had for me for a while, as I was trying to control joy and spiritual union and transcendence by "mastering" them! I wanted them to be complicated, so I could learn them instead of letting them be a gift from my creator I simply passively and gratefully received.

I try to make everything complicated, everything. But it isn't. Making it so may help others, but that's their path. I should not try to adopt or adapt to their behavior or belief systems.

It is as simple as my next breath and accepting the complete truth of myself and my situation in that breath. It has to be. Reality for me is that we all have feet of clay. I can accept this fact and not be surprised or bitter if my tendency to hero worship turns out badly.

I choose whom I trust. What a joy to finally learn it's okay to revise those choices as needed, and it is finally okay to trust myself.

Everything is changeable. That is good. A miracle could happen at any minute. I can start over every minute, if need be.

I don't need to borrow from others to grow. My faith is fully formed and continues to grow daily as I embrace and revel in the fact that I am not a mistake.

Everyone's journey is his or her own, but mine is about trusting my own experience more than the inconsistent words of others. Trusting my experience of God helps me to put more of my life and myself in his hands, day by day. I've been in his hands all along anyway. At long last, I have accepted this as the best possible thing for me and anyone else with whom I come into contact.

There is a reality I have long refused to accept: some people's words are not trustworthy. The fact I love them or respect them does not make their words honest or reliable. Just because someone speaks to me or for my benefit does not mean I need to regard it as a message from God.

It's up to me. I am not God, but what I believe about God is up to me, and no one else.

If God wants serenity and joy for me, who am I to be bitter and unhappy?

Why tear at myself or let others do it, intentionally or otherwise? If he loves me as I am, who am I to feel unloved?

I have not invented the Magna Carta here. So much of what

I discovered was not complicated. My intellect recognized it as relatively simple and filtered it, still looking for rules to follow, a burning bush and a choir of angels. Because I filtered it with my intellect, I still didn't get the message. I did not have any understanding of what I was experiencing and learning meant or how dramatically it could change my life.

I had to be desperate enough for it to reach and permeate my heart. Until I open my heart to an idea, I can't believe something and really know it. Then I can put it into practice in my life. For some, this insight has always been obvious, but I always missed the forest looking for the trees. It's that simple. Not easy, but simple. My making it more complicated does not make it more divine.

If God wants me to be free and forgiven, then why do I need to punish myself with judgmental people and unpleasant situations? I can't turn my back on the human race, but the one choice I will always have is what I let through the filter that guards my heart. It is where everything begins and ends.

No Deadline

The Israelites wandered in the desert for forty years on a trip that should have taken days. It took me even longer to find the Promised Land. So what? Not a single twist or turn was wasted. It took me as long as it took to get out of my head and the past and to start moving, not knowing the final destination. I was on God's timetable, not anyone else's.

What now?

No one knows what God wants for us but God, and sometimes us, if we are watching and listening. Figuring that out can't be done by committee.

But one thing I know for sure: My God speaks to me in ways only I can understand. Likely, you have a similar God. My God is a very dry British comedian. He is all about paradoxes and irony. That is where my answers always lie.

Why am I writing this book now? I couldn't write it before I stopped lying to myself and got free enough to write it.

In the end, it's all about courage: the courage to go on a Hero's Journey every day when we wake up. Faith in and optimism about the journey and trust that it is exactly what my Higher Power wants for me is my strength and source of power and peace. I will get to where I need to be when I need to get there. I can take one courageous step at a time, without knowing or analyzing all of the whats, whys, whos, and hows. I will transform gradually, as layer after layer of lies I tell myself and others are excavated and cleared away. This change will occur as God and I are ready.

Miracles are not produced by rules and tend to not respond to my timelines. The miracles in my life originally looked like insane whopping mistakes. I did something that didn't make sense to anyone, even me, and blessings began to flow.

No Shame

If our life is part of a plan, then our mistakes are part of the plan, aren't they?

The paradox of self-honesty and acceptance is that I need others to help me achieve it and maintain it. There has to be a village, a community, where there is true sanctuary in the traditional sense of the word. It has to be safe to "confess" and

CONCLUSION ❦ *(The Real Good News)*

let the ugly out, or we won't do it. True community is about joy and the freedom from fear and shame.

The only way to grow and transform and inspire is to get all of the poison out. To embrace this concept means a lifelong separation from and determination to be free of shame. If our life is to be a light for others and a glorification of God, shame has no place in it.

Some of us are more susceptible to shame and to pressures to conform than others. All of us need cheerleaders who recognize us and our efforts to live unabashed, and who encourage us to do so.

Church isn't bad.

But maybe the one we're in is bad for us at this particular moment in time. Today's religious institutions can be very different than the church some of us grew up with. Sometimes they can be really big business, and we can get a little lost in the hype.

Awareness of this had a hugely positive impact on my faith and spirituality. I realized I might as well trust myself and what I believed God was telling me. I was, in fact, trustworthy in navigating my own life.

My Hero's Journey was to excavate the person God created me to be out from under a mountain of false beliefs. I found sanctuary within myself and in the company of trusted friends, and I now hang onto it for dear life. I take this inner sanctuary with me everywhere I go, especially to church. I take Me to church and never let go of the idea my life is valuable and sacred, not just to me, but also to my Maker. I hang onto that and refuse to lose sight of it in the midst of pressures to conform.

Sanctuary

If you have read to this point, it should have become apparent I am not anti-church at all. I'm not saying, "Don't go to church." Instead I'm saying, "If it feels wrong for you, maybe it is. Go find the right one."

Further, "If lots of them feel wrong, then maybe it's time to find and claim your own spiritual identity first." My family and I have found a wonderful church and have been attending for decades. This church is a noisy, happy, functional spiritual family. A family who loves us unconditionally and we love every single member the same way. It is a place where grace abounds and is palpable. Joy and compassion bounce off of the walls like the beautiful notes the choir sings every Sunday.

I have loving and long friendships with congregants and pastors at several churches in the area, which I would never give up. It's because I changed~they didn't.

I did the heavy lifting first. I went on a lengthy pilgrimage from church to church before I finally figured out what I was in search of was my own spirit. The joyful and trusting child, confident in who she is.

Once I freed her, I had my full armor of God on and I was ready to return to my spiritual community. Because I had done this inner work, the return was so much sweeter. It really was coming home. I was whole and healed and sufficient in myself and could reach out to and embrace my community without fear of getting lost.

CONCLUSION ❦ *(The Real Good News)*

When looking for my church home, if I had to do it over again, I would ask the following questions at each and every stop on my pilgrimage:

>Does this look and act more like a family or a city?

>Is this structure limber enough to respond and adapt to me as an individual and to facilitate my journey and progression in the greater community of faith?

>Is this a place where I can find sanctuary?

>Can I stay here, and still be me?

Finally, if I felt especially broken, used, unworthy, and far from my God, I would look to myself first. I would resort to my own first aid kit before entrusting my spiritual psyche to anyone else.

My personal first aid kit would consist of my Bible and, even more importantly, my personal and past experience of my God. When has it been obvious my specific prayers have been answered? How were they answered? Did it look like something from a book? Was it like the prayers of the saints and disciples in the Bible?

No? Was there a pillar of smoke or a parting of a huge body of water? Did the help he sent look remotely like what I expected, or what the Church Elders thought it would? If it didn't look like what anyone else thought it should, I would ask myself, "Could they be wrong, instead of me?"

The lesson I learned the hard way is that no one, not a single person on this earth, can know me as well as my Creator knows me.

I don't know me as well as my Creator does, because I selectively hide or forget those parts too painful to face. So does everyone else.

Who can say the apparent setback of today won't turn out to be a miraculous and divine course correction? That has certainly turned out to be true for me. Why let anyone else put a label on your salvation or miracles or personal experience?

The even more brutal truth is I don't even know what is good for myself. Not really. I see things through my own particular filter. That may or may not be how they really are.

Knowing that, why would I turn my life and my precious soul over to someone else to evaluate? Why would I turn my life and my heart over to 500 or 5,000 others to evaluate? That is my Higher Power's job.

No Limits

The church isn't a building or a brand or a personality. Its bricks and mortar may be sanctified, but can't give us answers or guidance. The Bible calls it The Bride of Christ, with no concrete or "correct" location.

It is us. All of us. We each get a vote in what it should be and look like for us.

It is a place where we can come together and experience God, but it isn't God. It's not the only place we can find God. It's not the only way we can serve God.

It's best to know who we are before we walk in. To have

that in the back of our minds, in our ears, and in our hearts at all times. To know He has endowed us with splendor[57] and wants us to be undamned. To know we are undamned; know it, grab hold of this simple truth for dear life and never, ever let go.

> *The journey of a thousand miles begins with a single step.*
> ~ Lao Tsu

Onward.

CONCLUSION (*The Real Good News*)

Exit Sign[58]
Is a long green line
to freedom.
It's the taste of release,
the feeling of peace,
the sound of music and heavenly praise.
I can feel my arms raise
in exultation,
and the cool tingle of expectation,
the smell of fresh-cut grass and spring,
as I look out at the horizon and sing:
Amen.
An end.
And a beginning.

ACKNOWLEDGEMENTS

This book, and the new and improved version of me that resulted from writing it, could never have happened without the group of relentlessly loving, forgiving, and open-minded individuals who are my own personal sanctuary. It started 5 years ago as the idea of an escape. There are too many people who have listened, encouraged and guided over the years to name.

But you know who you are, because I tell you ad nauseum. My tribe. My cheerleaders. My truth-tellers. My mirror. You see value in me when I don't see it in myself. When there was nowhere else for me to go, I took you with me, and still do.

You tried to teach me what wisdom and confidence look like until I was ready to own them for myself. You listened to my ideas for this book and my fears and reasons for not writing it and patiently encouraged me. When I went on the self-imposed retreat that became the basis and the beginning of this story, I took you with me when I had no idea how I was going to do this. You patiently waited for my return to you, to sanity and to peace and joy.

To my parents, for putting my own happiness ahead of their own and understanding I needed to write this to fully become me. Thanks for never telling me it was too late for me to grow up or follow my dreams.

Thanks to my husband and children for going with me on this long pilgrimage and for putting up with my frequent, sudden, and lengthy Starbucks Writing Sabbaticals.

UNDAMNED

Thanks to Nathan Brown, Poet Laureate of Oklahoma, who made it okay and even fun for me to start writing poems in my middle years. If he had not encouraged me to write those first poems, I would have written nothing at all.

Thanks to Taylor Gahm for listening and encouraging and telling me my ideas were not crazy. Mark Mitchell, thank you, thank you, thank you for recognizing this as my baby and for seeing the beauty in her. You made her clearer, brighter, bolder, and more beautiful with your gentle and respectful edits. Thanks also to Jenny Meadows and Cynthia Stone for their tireless edits and their patience as I pushed back and argued.

Thanks to the Purcells and to Laity Lodge for providing a place for art, serenity, and the holy to converge. For me, that is where it all begins and ends.

FOOTNOTES

1. © L.E. Kinzie, 2012. All rights reserved.
2. © L.E. Kinzie, 2013. All rights reserved.
3. Rob Bell, *Love Wins: A Book about Heaven, Hell, and the Fate of Every Person Who Ever Lived*, New York: Harper One, 2011.
4. Rob Bell and Don Golden, *Jesus Wants to Save Christians: A Manifesto for the Church in Exile*, Grand Rapids: Yates & Yates, 2008.
5. Matthew 23:27, NIV.
6. Matthew 19:20-22, NIV.
7. Isaiah 55:8, NIV
8. Peter Rollins, *How (Not) to Speak of God*, Brewster, Mass.: Paraclete, 2006.
9. Ephesians 2:10, NIV
10. © L.E. Kinzie, 2011. All rights reserved.
11. Rob Bell, *Love Wins*.
12. Proverbs 4:23, NIV
13. Rollins, How (Not) to Speak of God.
14. Emmet Fox, Around the Year with Emmet Fox: A Book of Daily Readings, New York: Harper, 1958.
15. 1 Corinthians 13:4-8, NIV
16. Ephesians 5:22, NIV
17. Exodus 20:14, NIV
18. My interpretation of 1 Corinthians 13:7
19. Exodus 20:16, KJV
20. After a number of teenagers died in collisions with vehicles and trains after drinking legally at local bars, the Dram Shop laws were enacted. They made a bar liable if it continued to serve patrons who were clearly drunk. In the same general timeframe, Mothers Against Drunk Driving (MADD) was formed and became a huge force of awareness and reform.
21. Parts of Psalm 139, from Eugene H. Peterson, *The Message Remix:*

The Bible in Contemporary Language, Colorado Springs: NavPress, 2003.
22. Isaiah 30:15, NIV
23. Proverbs 4:23, NIV
24. Luke 17:21, NIV
25. Isaiah 54:10, NIV
26. Ephesians 6:13-18, NIV
27. 1 Corinthians 10:14-15, NIV
28. Mark 2:22, NIV
29. *The High Calling Daily Reflection* by Mark D. Roberts, Tuesday, August 6, 2013
30. Isaiah 55:11, NIV
31. Exodus 32:1, NIV
32. Exodus 32:3,4, NIV
33. Ephesians 6:13-18, NIV
34. Ibid, 6:13-18
35. Parts of Psalm 139, from Eugene H. Peterson, *The Message Remix: The Bible in Contemporary Language*, Colorado Springs: NavPress, 2003.
36. Matthew 22: 36-40, NIV
37. Matthew 10:28, from Eugene H. Peterson, *The Message Remix: The Bible in Contemporary Language*, Colorado Springs: NavPress, 2003
38. 1 John 4:18, NIV
39. 1 John 4:20, NIV
40. Habakkuk 2:18, NIV
41. Jonah 2:8, NIV
42. Exodus 20:3, NIV
43. 1st Corinthians 1:19, NIV
44. 1st Corinthians 1:21, NIV
45. Psalm 111:10, NIV
46. Bill Rollins, *How (Not) to Speak of God*.
47. U.S Dept. of health and Human Services, Children's Bureau acf.hhs.

http://www.gov/programs/cb stats
48. Pia Mellody, with Andrea Wells Miller and Keith Miller, *Facing Codependence,* ©2003, Harper One
49. Ibid.
50. Ibid.
51. Ibid.
52. Psalm 27, NIV
53. Psalm 139, NIV
54. Isaiah 41:10, NIV
55. Psalm 139, NIV
56. Best of Spa Music: Yoga, Meditation, Massage and Spa.
57. Isaiah 55:5, NIV
58. ©L.E. Kinzie, 2010, all rights reserved

www.ingramcontent.com/pod-product-compliance
Lightning Source LLC
Chambersburg PA
CBHW060750050426
42449CB00008B/1344